EXISTENCE,

BEING

AND

GOD

An

Introduction

to the Philosophical
Theology of
John Macquarrie

EXISTENCE, BEING AND GOD

An Introduction to the Philosophical Theology of John Macquarrie

Eugene Thomas Long

Paragon House Publishers

New York

Published in the United States by
Paragon House Publishers
2 Hammarskjold Plaza
New York, NY 10017

ISBN: 0-913729-02-7 (Hardbound)
       0-913729-08-6 (Softbound)

Library of Congress Cataloging in Publication Data

Long, Eugene Thomas.
    Existence, Being, and God.

    Bibliography: p.
    Includes index.
    1. Macquarrie, John.   I. Title.
BX4827.M25L661984   230′.044′0924   84-16566

TO MY PARENTS

Eugene Thomas Long, Jr. and Emily Barker Long

CONTENTS

PREFACE

The aim of this work is to provide an introduction to the philosophical theology of John Macquarrie. In his proposal for a new style of philosophical or natural theology, Macquarrie is influenced primarily by the existentialist theology of Rudolf Bultmann and the existential-ontological philosophy of Martin Heidegger. The central issue which guides Macquarrie's thought is the expression of faith in God from within an existentialist framework. Theological inquiry begins, according to Macquarrie, with the question of human existence. Theology, however, is also concerned wiith the question of God. Macquarrie's new style of natural theology begins with describing and interpreting the structures of existence and Being and places the distinctively religious concepts on the ontological map of the Being of human existence.

The first chapter of this book is an intellectual biography showing the development of Macquarrie's approach to natural theology and focusing on the central issue which guides his thought. Following this, Macquarrie's understanding of the Being of human existence is analyzed. In his analysis of human existence, Macquarrie shows the polarities and disorders in human existence which point to religious faith's understanding of the meaningfulness of existence and Being. Succeeding chapters are concerned with the content of faith, the knowledge of God and the meaning and truth of the language of faith.

This book was in press when I received a copy of Macquarrie's recently published Gifford Lectures, delivered at the University of Saint Andrews in the 1983–84 academic session. The title of the published version of these lectures is *In Search of Deity: An Essay in Dialectical Theology*. In his earier work Macquarrie refers to himself as a panentheist. In his most recent book, however, he prefers the expression "dialectical theism." He uses this expression to more clearly distinguish his position from pantheism and classical theism. Dialectical theism stresses that his view is a species of theism and the adjective "dialectical" makes clear his intent to avoid the one-sidedness of classical theism in which the ideas of divine immanence and divine participation in history were treated inadequately.

ix

Although I must take responsibility for the interpretation of Macquarrie's thought provided in this book, I want to thank him for the valuable discussions that I have had with him concerning portions of this book. He and his wife have always been most generous with their time and hospitalty. I also want to thank Bonnie Lane who, more than once, has seen portions of this book through her typewriter. As always I cannot find adequate words to express my indebtedness to Lyn, Scott and Kathy whose tolerance and understanding seem unlimited.

The University of South Carolina   Eugene Thomas Long

ACKNOWLEDGMENTS

The author gratefully acknowledges assistance from the University of South Carolina Research and Productive Scholarship Committee for funds which facilitated the completion of this book.

Some portions of this book are quoted and/or paraphrased from essays previously published by the author. The author is grateful for permission to use material from the following: "Macquarrie on 'God Exists'," *International Journal for Philosophy of Religion,* 10:4 (1979); "John Macquarrie on God," *Perspectives in Religious Studies,* 7:3 (1980); "Being and Thinking," *The Southern Journal of Philosophy,* 9:2 (1971); "John Macquarrie on Language, Being and God," *The Review of Metaphysics,* 30:3 (1976); "John Macquarrie on Ultimate Reality and Meaning," *Ultimate Reality and Meaning,* 6:4 (1983).

The author is indebted to the following for permissions to quote from the following books: John Macquarrie, *Principles of Christian Theology,* Second Edition. Copyright © 1966, 1967 by John Macquarrie (New York: Charles Scribner's Sons, 1977 and London: SCM Press, Ltd., 1977). Reprinted with permission of Charles Scribner's Sons and SCM Press, Ltd. John Macquarrie, *Thinking About God.* Copyright © 1975 by SCM Press, Ltd. (London: SCM Press, Ltd., 1975 and New York: Harper and Row, Publishers, 1975). Reprinted with permission of SCM Press, Ltd. and Harper and Row, Publishers. John Macquarrie, *In Search of Humanity.* Copyright © 1982 by John Macquarrie (London: SCM Press, Ltd., 1982 and New York: The Crossroad Publishing Company, 1983). Reprinted with permission of SCM Press, Ltd., and The Crossroad Publishing Company. John Macquarrie, *God-Talk.* Copyright © 1967 by SCM Press, Ltd. (London: SCM Press, Ltd., 1967 and New York: Harper and Row, Publishers, 1967). Reprinted with permission of John Macquarrie, Harper and Row, Publishers and SCM Press, Ltd. Martin Heidegger, *Being and Time. Translated by John Macquarrie and Edward Robinson. Copyright © 1962 by SCM Press, Ltd. (London: SCM Press, Ltd., 1962, Oxford: Basil Blackwell, 1967 and New York: Harper and Row, Publishers, Inc., 1962) Reprinted with permission of Harper and Row, Publishers, Basil Blackwell, and SCM Press, Ltd.*

1

———

A NEW STYLE
OF NATURAL
THEOLOGY

THE CENTRAL PHILOSOPHICAL AND THEOLOGICAL PROBLEM FOR
John Macquarrie, since the time of his dissertation on Martin
Heidegger and Rudolf Bultmann, has been the expression of
faith in God within an existentialist framework. Theological
inquiry begins, according to Macquarrie, with the question of
human existence. Theology, however, must also concern itself
with the question of God. It is the transition from statements
about human existence to statements about God that lies at the
heart of Macquarrie's own philosophical theology.

John Macquarrie was born on June 27, 1919, in Renfew,
Scotland, to John and Robina (McInnes) Macquarrie. Renfew
lies on the Clyde River approximately six miles from Glasgow,
Scotland's industrial giant. Macquarrie's grandfather, who
spoke Gaelic, came from the Island of Islay to work on the
Clydeside. Macquarrie's father was a skilled shipyard worker
and an elder in the Presbyterian church. Macquarrie's upbring-
ing fostered in him a sense of deep religious commitment that
has always been balanced by tolerance and an openness toward
others. He recognized early both the importance of religious
conviction and the legitimacy of religious diversity. Indeed,

(1)

both a spirit of charity and a depth of conviction equally characterize his work.

Macquarrie was educated at Paisley Grammar School and then at the University of Glasgow, where he received the M.A. degree in philosophy in 1940. He studied under Charles Arthur Campbell, Professor of Logic and Rhetoric, to whom he dedicated *Existentialism* (1972). Campbell is sometimes listed among the absolute idealists, but he does not fit easily into the idealist mold. He does not, for example, accept any of the metaphysical arguments for the identification of reality with Absolute Mind or Spirit. He has also said that were he not convinced of the validity of the epistemology of idealism, he would probably disclaim the idealist label altogether. (He is referring to the so-called judgment theory of cognition, which sees cognition as a process of ideally characterizing an objective, independent reality.)[1]

In his first book, *Skepticism and Construction* (1931), Campbell explored the idea of the Absolute as suprarational in terms of moral and religious experience and intellectual understanding. In his Gifford Lectures, delivered at the University of St. Andrews in 1953–1954 and 1954–1955 and later published as *On Selfhood and Godhood,* Campbell further advanced some of his ideas on natural theology. Religious experience, Campbell argues in these lectures, finds its developed theoretical expression in theism, but rational theism, which attempts to apply attributes to God in a literal way, is internally inconsistent and untenable. Campbell claims that Rudolf Otto has shown that suprarational or symbolic theism "is the only form of theism that is in accord with the full complexity of actual religious experience."[2] The qualities that are ascribed to God, Campbell continues, should be understood as analogical symbols of the divine nature by which we deny and affirm God's positive content. This dialectic of affirmation and denial does not lead, however, to merely subjective claims, for symbolic knowledge is distinguished from mere nescience and from knowledge in the strict sense. Campbell argues further that philosophy can offer some corroboration for religious claims through metaphysical inquiry and through our understanding of the moral order by which we are led to a view of ultimate reality that is at least consistent with the religious view of God.

Perhaps one should not suggest too much in the way of

Campbell's direct influence on Macquarrie's thought. Macquarrie has great respect and affection for Campbell and admits of a continuing influence, but it should be pointed out that Macquarrie had become a lecturer at the University of Glasgow and had published his first book before Campbell's major contribution to natural theology, *On Selfhood and Godhood,* appeared. Nevertheless, once some important differences are granted, interesting parallels can be drawn between Campbell and Macquarrie regarding the limits of rational theism, the nature of religious language, and the roles of philosophy and theology in relation to the centrality of experience in religion. Also, Campbell may have helped to provide a receptive yet critical framework for Macquarrie's reading of Bultmann and Heidegger, the two major influences on Macquarrie's thought.

Following his studies in philosophy, Macquarrie studied theology at Glasgow, completing the B.D. degree in 1943. He served for several years as chaplain in the British army and became minister of St. Ninian's Church, Brechin (Church of Scotland), in 1948, a position he held until 1953, when he became lecturer in Systematic Theology at the University of Glasgow. Macquarrie studied for the Ph.D. degree at Glasgow under Ian Henderson at a time when the so-called Barthian revolution was having a significant impact on theology in the English-speaking world. Henderson had studied philosophy at the University of Edinburgh under Norman Kemp Smith and A. E. Taylor and theology under John Baillie and Hugh Ross Mackintosh. He had also studied at Basle under Karl Barth. Macquarrie has described Henderson as a child of the Enlightenment and a foe of Romanticism.[3] Henderson had great respect for Barth and, with James Haire, had translated Barth's Gifford Lectures, but he criticized Barth's theological position and looked to the work of Rudolf Bultmann in his quest for intellectual integrity in theology. Following the publication in 1948 of *Can Two Walk Together?,* a study of the foundations of morality, Henderson published *Myth in the New Testament* (1952), which introduced to the English-speaking world the controversy over Bultmann's program of demythologizing. In the last section of that book, Henderson deals critically with what he believes is the inadequacy of Bultmann's position on the historical Jesus; he raises the question whether the myths of the New Testament can be fully translated into the language of human existence without some loss. This was a question that Macquarrie himself was to take up.

Henderson was completing *Myth in the New Testament* while Macquarrie was writing his dissertation, which was completed in 1954 and published in 1955 as *An Existentialist Theology: A Comparison of Heidegger and Bultmann*. *An Existentialist Theology* was one of the first volumes published in the well-known Library of Philosophy and Theology begun by Ronald Gregor Smith when he was director of the SCM Press in London. Gregor Smith, himself a student of the Enlightenment and much influenced by Bultmann, joined Henderson and Macquarrie on the faculty at Glasgow in 1956. In 1962 Macquarrie became professor of systematic theology at Union Theological Seminary in New York, a position he retained until 1970, when he was appointed Lady Margaret Professor of Divinity at Oxford University.

While at Union, he met John Knox, who at 62 was in the process of changing from the Methodist to the Episcopal Church. Macquarrie had been attracted to the Anglican Communion from about the age of 17, but in deference to his Scottish family had been reluctant to change. Bultmann's treatment of the ideas of community and Church had seemed inadequate to Macquarrie, and he has spoken of his indebtedness to Knox's profound insights into the nature of the Church. Macquarrie attended Knox's ordination to the priesthood in December 1962. In 1963 Macquarrie joined the Anglican Communion and was ordained by the bishop of New York on June 16, 1965.

In *An Existentialist Theology,* Macquarrie's primary intent is to contribute to the understanding of the influence of existentialist philosophy on contemporary theological thought. The book is largely expository in character and reveals the clarity and crispness of style for which Macquarrie has become widely recognized. In his agreements with and criticisms of Bultmann, however, there are indications of how Macquarrie's own ideas were developing. Macquarrie accepts Bultmann's proposition that the message of the New Testament can be made intelligible only in the context of an understanding of human existence in which the life of faith is seen as a real possibility within the range of human possibilities. The analysis of the range of human or existential possibilities is understood by Macquarrie to be the task of philosophy, a task he calls ontological or pre-theological. Like

Bultmann, he looks primarily to Heidegger for this analysis. Macquarrie argues, however, that in calling for a translation of all statements about transcendence into statements about human existence, Bultmann does not do justice to the other pole of theology to which Bultmann also appeals, the activity of God in Christ. Theology, says Macquarrie,

> is concerned not only with statements about human existence but with statements about God and his activity as well—transcendent statements, if you like, which, because we lack categories for the understanding of transcendent being as such, can only be expressed in symbolic or mythical form. . . . Just as Heidegger intended to pass beyond the analysis of human existence to the quest for being in the widest sense, so theology cannot rest in existential statements, but must go on to speak of God and the transcendent—though in both cases the question of man's existence certainly appears to me to be the right starting-point for the inquiry.[4]

This concern with the relation between statements about human existence and about God is the focus of Macquarrie's second book, *The Scope of Demythologizing,* published in 1960. It is a revision and expansion of lectures delivered at Union Theological Seminary in March in 1957, and Macquarrie regards it as a companion to *An Existentialist Theology.* In the book he evaluates what he takes to be the central problem in Bultmann's theology, the limits inherent in the program of demythologizing. On the one hand, Bultmann seeks to translate fully the teaching of the New Testament into statements about human existence. On the other hand, he insists on speaking of God's decisive act in Christ. Macquarrie questions whether these two aspects of Bultmann's theology can be integrated. Although he defends Bultmann against those critics who argue that the kerygma is lost through the program of demythologizing and those critics who would merge theology with a philosophy of existence and thus devalue discussion of an act of God, Macquarrie acknowledges the value of such criticisms in pointing out, directly or indirectly, the limitations in the demythologizing program.

In his discussion of Bultmann's program of demythologizing, Macquarrie also insists, in a way that Bultmann does not, that there must be a "minimum core of factuality" in the Christian faith.[5] Faith as authentic understanding must be supplemented by an appeal to the historical Jesus. Schubert Ogden, in his widely read *Christ Without Myth,* has challenged Macquarrie on this point, claiming that his argument is fallacious and that Macquarrie breaches the Reformation principles of *sola gratia-sola fide.*[6] Macquarrie, however, does not intend to make theology dependent on historical research or to argue that historical research may provide a proof of faith.

He does want to insist that Christian faith have some empirical anchor, without which faith is likely to be little more than an idealistic possibility. His reference to a minimum core of factuality amounts to an assertion that at the heart of the Christian religion is an actual historical instance of that pattern of life proclaimed as a possibility for us, in the kerygma, in the notions of dying to one form of life and rising in another. Macquarrie would admit that this pattern of life cannot be shown with certainty to have been realized in history, but he does argue that it has remained a constant in the varied findings of historical research, and he believes we can have reasonable confidence that the commitment of faith is to a realistic possibility of existence.[7]

Macquarrie's insistence on an empirical anchorage for Christian faith is closely tied to his insistence that faith is inseparable from questions of truth and justification. He argues in his later work that although natural theology cannot offer a proof for faith, "any faith must let itself be exposed to the observable facts of the world in which we live. The business of natural theology is to show that these facts are not incompatible with the convictions of faith, and may even tend to confirm these convictions."[8] To suggest, as Ogden does, that Macquarrie breaches the principles of *sola gratia-sola fide* is, one suspects, to confuse the doctrine of salvation by faith alone with an epistemological doctrine that faith is a commitment requiring no justification.

At the heart of the issues with which Macquarrie is struggling—the relation of faith to history, the limits to translating the teaching of the New Testament into statements about human existence, and the truth of faith—is the larger problem of religious language. Specifically, the question that guides Macquarrie's investigations is: How is one to speak of God from within an existentialist framework? Jaspers' cipher language, Heidegger's phenomenology of discourse, and Bultmann's analysis of mythical, symbolic, and analogical language all suggest the importance of language in the existentialist tradition. However, little attention has been given by the existentialists to the logic of language, a task that has been central to much twentieth-century British and American analytical philosophy. Macquarrie considers it unfortunate that although the existential and analytical philosophers have many roots in common, they have tended to work independently of one another.

In *The Scope of Demythologizing,* Macquarrie shows his acquaintance with the work of such philosophers of language as Wittgenstein, Ayer, Braithwaite, Crombie, Wilson, Ian Ramsey, and William Zuurdeeg, as well as with the work of his own teacher, Campbell, who had discussed symbolic and analogical language in his Gifford lectures. But he is primarily concerned with outlining Heidegger's analysis of the relation between language and existence. With this book, Macquarrie also begins a dialogue with analytical philosophers and lays the groundwork for his later efforts to develop a logic of the language of religion. In particular, he responds to Ronald Hepburn's perceptive essay, "Demythologizing and the Problem of Validity," in which Hepburn applies the analytical approach to Bultmann's existential interpretation. If our speech is to be clarified, our theories to be made consistent, and the problem of validity to be dealt with adequately, Macquarrie suggests, we need the analytical philosopher's analysis of the logic of language, in addition to existential analysis.

For Macquarrie, the language of religion is always bound up with the speaker, and an understanding of the speaker is therefore central to understanding his language, a point we shall treat in greater detail in Chapter 5. Heidegger, in his study of the discourse situation in *Being and Time,* calls attention to the existential matrix of meanings in words, something that is forgotten when language is analyzed independently of the context in which people express their being in the world. Abstract languages are suitable, even necessary, in many fields, including the natural sciences, but Macquarrie, like Heidegger, believes that since we relate to reality in a variety of ways, and since our more abstract languages do not fully reflect our primary relations to reality, one function of philosophy should be to preserve the existential force of language. Scientific language, suggests Macquarrie, is a depersonalized language; the speaker for the most part can be ignored. There are, however, more personal forms of language in which man expresses himself, "where the relation between what is said, and the person who says it is so close that any linguistic analysis would need to be correlated with an existential analysis."[9] Macquarrie considers religious language just such a personal language form, and he understands Bultmann's program of demythologizing to be an effort to interpret myth as personal language. While acknowledging Bultmann's existential analysis of the language of religion as a powerful tool, however, Macquarrie argues that his analysis of the logic of language is limited to brief, suggestive, and at times confused remarks and that a more developed logical analysis is required. Much of the confusion can be attributed to Bultmann's early definition of myth, which would seem to include all talk of transcendence, and to his failure to distinguish adequately between mythological, symbolic, and analogical talk of God. In *The Scope of Demythologizing,* Macquarrie provides the beginnings of a reconstruction of Bultmann's theory of religious language. Later Macquarrie develops his own theory in more detail. This will be discussed further in Chapter 5.

Macquarrie agrees with Hepburn that Bultmann defines mythical language too broadly, with the result that were he consistent, Bultmann would eliminate all talk of God. Bultmann, however, does not eliminate talk of God. In spite of calling for a demythologizing of all mythical talk of God, he wants to make a place for symbolic and analogical talk of God. Unfortunately, he fails to draw clear distinctions between the terms "myth," "symbol," and "analogy," and interpreters of Bultmann tend to be left bewildered. The central problem, according to Macquarrie, is that Bultmann does not make clear the distinction between the literal and the symbolic in mythical talk. We become aware of myth as myth when its symbolic character is recognized, when the imagery is recognized as imagery. But this, argues Macquarrie, leaves a need to develop a more consciously conceptual form of language, a language that is more universal in character, more available to understanding beyond the limits of our particular historical traditions. Although Bultmann's discussion of these issues is without clarity and precision, Macquarrie believes that the kinds of distinctions he is drawing are at least implicit in Bultmann's work.[10]

In his analysis of Bultmann's theory of religious language, Macquarrie abandons Bultmann's original definition of myth and reconstructs it, drawing more careful distinctions between mythical, symbolic, and analogical statements and suggesting that Bultmann does not in fact intend to reduce all mythical statements in religion to existential statements. Bultmann intends at least to make a place for talk of God as well as human existence. If, however, this much can be granted to Bultmann, there is still the problem put sharply by Hepburn concerning how statements about God manage to *refer*, how one manages to escape from a subjectivist circle and say anything about God. Macquarrie does not at this point provide a fully developed answer to this question, but he does set up the fundamentals of an approach that he will later develop in more detail. Since God, according to Macquarrie, is not an entity like other entities in the world, religious statements about God cannot refer to some state of affairs the way factual statements refer to such states of affairs. For this reason, a correspondence theory of truth is ruled out. If, writes Macquarrie, "anything can be said for the validity of religious statements, it must come from the discrimination and analysis of religious experience itself."[11]

Macquarrie is appealing here to Heidegger's view that truth consists in making unconcealed what is being discoursed about, suggesting that religious statements are intended to disclose the being of human existence and its relation to Being itself understood as gracious. The claims of religious statements understood in this manner could not be proved in any ordinary sense, but a reasonable interpretation of the experience of existence and Being can be attempted and the adequacy of the interpretation assessed.

From 1953, when he began lecturing at the University of Glasgow, to 1962, when he gave his inaugural lecture at Union Theological Seminary, Macquarrie devoted most of his scholarly efforts to the translation, exposition, and criticism of the work of others. In addition to the two volumes already discussed, in 1962 he published with Edward Robinson of the University of Kansas an English translation of Martin Heidegger's *Sein und Zeit*. In 1957 Macquarrie was asked by Harper and Row to write a history of religious thought in the twentieth century. Completed in 1961, this was published in 1963 under the title *Twentieth Century Religious Thought*. Virtually an encyclopedia of the work of more than 150 philosophers and theologians, *Twentieth-Century Religious Thought* testifies to Macquarrie's remarkable ability to sum up the essential aspects of a theory or system of thought in a few words. Macquarrie's critical commentary also provides a guide to the maturation and development of his own thought.

In 1962 Macquarrie was invited to write a systematic theology, published four years later as *Principles of Christian Theology*. A revised edition appeared in 1977. Also in 1962, Macquarrie gave the Hastie Lectures at the University of Glasgow on "The Problem of Theological Language." The theme was further developed at several universities in the United States, and resulted in 1967 in the publication of *God-Talk: An Examination of the Language and Logic of Theology*.

Although Macquarrie is concerned with a number of philosophical and theological problems, the central issue in these and subsequent volumes is the transition from talk of human existence to talk of Being or God. On this issue, it is Bultmann who is Macquarrie's principal guide to understanding the New Testament, and it is Heidegger's method and analysis of the meaning of existence and Being that provide Macquarrie with the basis for a viable twentieth-century style of natural or philosophical theology, his most significant contribution to date.

Traditionally, natural theology referred to knowledge of God arrived at by reason alone, and revealed theology referred to knowledge of God through his revelation of himself. These two forms of knowledge were considered separate and distinct but also supplemental to one another. According to St. Thomas Aquinas, religious knowledge could be achieved by both "an ascent through creatures to the knowledge of God by the natural light of reason" and "a descent of divine truth by revelation to us; truth exceeding human understanding; truth accepted, not as demonstrated to sight, but as orally delivered for belief."[12] Although there were shifts in emphasis between natural and revealed theology, this distinction between them was maintained for the most part until the time of Kant and Hume, whose philosophical criticisms of the traditional arguments for the existence of God called into question the very basis of natural theology. And even if the traditional arguments could be considered valid, an unbridgeable gap remains, according to many contemporary thinkers, between the God of natural theology and the God of religious faith. The theological claim (carried to its extreme) that man's reason is bound by his sin or his finiteness and the notion that any knowledge of God lies with the initiative of God (man being merely a passive recipient of God's revelation of himself) further reduce the possibility of linking the world of ordinary experience with the world of faith.

To accept such a conclusion would relegate religion to a private world of revelation and unjustifiable faith. It has been widely recognized that if religious faith is to have any relevance to modern culture, some foundation is needed that would permit one to relate the claims of religious knowledge to other types of knowledge. Given the significant criticisms leveled at it, traditional natural theology has not been able to provide such a foundation; a new form of natural theology is required. In Macquarrie's words,

> The basic function of natural theology may be something quite different from devising a watertight proof, and the fact that our traditional natural theology has been formulated in terms of logical demonstration may be due only to the operation of certain historical and cultural factors in the West. We could say that the function of natural theology was to provide a connection between our ordinary everyday discourse about the world or even our scientific discourse on the one side, and theological discourse on the other.[13]

Macquarrie is proposing a new style of natural theology, one that "would press back beyond the traditional arguments to examine the conviction that lay behind them."[14] Macquarrie's new style of natural theology is founded on Heidegger's analysis of the experience of existence and Being. Indeed, Macquarrie refers to Heidegger's philosophy as offering a natural religion or theology that can be considered in its own right and that might be satisfying to those not attracted to institutional religion.[15]

A natural theology of this type does not set out to prove

anything in the strict sense, but intends to reveal the context of religious faith. This approach is existential rather than rationalistic in the narrow sense. It appeals to a broad understanding of our existence in the world and takes account of our moods and feelings, which for Macquarrie have a role in disclosing in some cognitive way the Being of our existence in the world. The primary methods are those of description and interpretation. Natural theology—or philosophical theology, as Macquarrie seems to prefer to call it—uses as its starting point a secular description of the structures of existence and Being and attempts to place the distinctively religious concepts, such as grace, faith, and God, on the ontological map of the Being of human existence.

With this approach, the traditional distinction between a natural and a revealed knowledge of God is essentially abandoned. Natural theology now appeals to a general possibility of revelation rather than a speculative metaphysics. Further, natural theology is understood not as a kind of preliminary step to revealed theology but as an accompaniment to it. This new style of natural theology is a critical reflection that moves freely between the assertions of religious faith and the secular understanding of existence and Being in an effort to relate and reconcile them.[16] As Macquarrie puts it:

> Though it (natural theology) could not establish a religious faith, it can support one. The point is that any faith must let itself be exposed to the observable facts of the world in which we live. The business of natural theology is to show that these facts are not incompatible with the convictions of faith, and may even tend to confirm these convictions."[17]

Macquarrie's new style of natural theology is thus intended to provide a bridge between our ordinary ways of understanding ourselves in the world and faith's understanding of human existence in relation to Being or God. In his inaugural lecture at Union Theological Seminary, Macquarrie said: "If man is, as Christianity asserts, a creature of God and dependent on him, then this should show itself in a study of man. It should be possible to see man as fragmentary and incomplete in himself, so that we are pointed to God, and if we can see man in this way, then we can go on to a fuller understanding of him in his relation to God."[18] Acknowledging the polarities and tensions inherent in our understanding of human existence—the focus of the next chapter—will provide the grounds for making the transition to the wider range of Being or God.

Notes

1. See C. A. Campbell, *In Defense of Free Will* (London: Allen and Unwin, 1967), p. 241; and *On Selfhood and Godhood* (London: Allen and Unwin, 1957), pp. 55–72.
2. *On Selfhood and Godhood,* p. 326.
3. John Macquarrie, *Thinking About God* (New York: Harper and Row, 1975), pp. 205–206.
4. John Macquarrie, *An Existentialist Theology* (London: SCM Press, 1955), pp. 244–45.
5. John Macquarrie, *The Scope of Demythologizing* (London: SCM Press, 1960), pp. 90ff. Cited hereinafter as *Scope*.
6. See Schubert Ogden, *Christ Without Myth* (New York: Harper and Row, 1961), pp. 165–81; and Macquarrie's response in *Studies in Christian Existentialism* (London: SCM Press, 1966), pp. 156–67. Cited hereinafter as *Studies*.
7. *Studies*, pp. 139–50. *Principles of Christian Theology,* Second Edition (New York: Charles Scribner's Sons, 1977), pp. 273ff. Cited hereinafter as *Principles*.
8. John Macquarrie, *God-Talk. An Examination of the Language and Logic of Theology* (New York: Harper and Row, 1967), p. 234. Cited hereinafter as *God-Talk*.
9. *Scope,* p. 127.
10. *Scope,* p. 206.
11. *Scope,* p. 217.
12. Thomas Aquinas, *Of God and His Creatures.* An annotated translation of *Summa Contra Gentiles* by Joseph Rickaby (Maryland: The Carroll Press, 1950), Book IV, Chapter 1, p. 339.
13. *Thinking About God,* p. 137.
14. *Principles,* p. 56.
15. *Studies,* p. 57.
16. *Thinking About God,* p. 140.
17. *God-Talk,* p. 234.
18. *Studies,* p. 5.

2

EXISTENCE
AND
BEING

THE CENTRAL PROBLEM FOR MACQUARRIE, AGAIN, IS HOW ONE can talk of God within an existentialist framework, how one can make the transition from statements about human existence to statements about God. For theology to begin with the experience of existence and Being, an appropriate method is required, and Macquarrie finds this in phenomenology. Through describing and interpreting the meaning of the experience of existence and Being, Macquarrie shows how the religious categories can be understood in a secular context. This approach is based on two basic beliefs.

First, Macquarrie believes that the traditional arguments for the existence of God have been treated independently of the context in which they were developed. As a result, we have missed the fact that conviction about the reality of God preceded these proofs, which were developed in meditations on this conviction. When the arguments are understood in context, it can be argued that theists were not intending to offer proofs in the strict sense. Rather, they were tracing patterns in their own experience in the world to discover rational support for their convictions and to account for evidence that seemed to counter these convictions. One purpose of Macquarrie's philosophical theology, then, is to get back to the experience and convictions that underlie the traditional arguments for the existence of God. He turns to existential analysis for the means of elucidating the basic patterns of experience that lead to religious convictions.

Second, as we saw in Chapter 1, Macquarrie believes that if man is in some sense a creature of God and dependent on God, as Christian theology asserts, an analysis of the Being of human existence should point us to God. Here too existential analysis should provide both an understanding of God in relation to human existence and a basis for a fuller understanding of man in his relation to God. In describing the basic structures of man's experience in the world, one should expect to discover that in some sense man is incomplete in himself and that he points beyond himself to God.

In describing man's experience of existence and Being, Macquarrie is not claiming to demonstrate that man's understanding of himself requires God, although we shall see in Chapter 4 that he does offer a cumulative argument for belief in God. Macquarrie is rather providing a phenomenology or description and interpretation of man's experience of existence and Being to let us see the phenomenon as it actually is, without concealments and distortions. In this he echoes Heidegger, who says that phenomenology means "to let that which shows itself be seen from itself in the very way in which it shows itself from itself."[1]

Presumably no description we make can be completely free of all the presuppositions or interpretive schemes we bring with us to experience. However, as Ninian Smart suggests, we can at least distinguish between highly ramified and relatively unramified interpretations. Macquarrie's phenomenological approach contributes to his description of the experience of existence and Being a basis for evaluating such interpretive schemes as true or false, that is, as adequate or inadequate to the data of experience.

Macquarrie begins his analysis of the experience of existence and Being with a distinction familiar to readers of existential philosophy, between the existence of man and the existence of objects. In traditional language, to talk about man's existence is to talk about his thatness (that he is) rather than his essence or whatness (what he is). In this case, however, the distinction between the existence of rocks and the existence of persons either is not made or is left ambiguous. It is the traditional way of talking about existence that makes puzzling Heidegger's remark that *"The 'essence' of Dasein lies in its existence."*[2] In speaking of Dasein or the Being of human existence, however, Heidegger is careful to distinguish between "existence" in its traditional sense, where it is applied indiscriminately to persons and rocks, and "existence" as he uses the term in reference to humans. When we speak of the existence of something in the traditional sense, we mean that we come across something in the world. For this sense, Heidegger uses the term "presence-at-hand" (*Vorhandenheit*). He reserves "existence" (*Existenz*) for that kind of being that is peculiar to humans. To say of Dasein that its essence lies in its existence is to say that it is an entity for which its being is an issue, that it is constituted by its possible ways of being.

Not all existentialists distinguish between the existence of objects and the existence of persons the same way Heidegger does. Generally speaking, however, existentialist thinkers use "existence" to single out the particular kind of being that is exemplified in man. Macquarrie suggests that in contrast to other entities, man is open to his being. Man not only is, but also is aware of who or what he is and who or what he may become. In Heidegger's words, "We are ourselves the entities to be analyzed. The Being of any such entity is *in each case mine*. These entities, in their Being, comport themselves towards their Being. . . . *Being is that which is an issue for every such entity.*"[3] Human existence, understood in this way, is held to be disclosed to itself as unfinished, never complete in its being. Man is not constituted by some properties assigned to him but is always projecting himself into his possible ways of being.

Human existence is not just one entity among others. For certain purposes in the natural and social sciences, we may represent persons in some statistical manner, and it may be a matter of indifference which individuals are selected for study. Indeed, many of these studies are based on a kind of sameness between experimental and control groups. But one needs to keep in mind that in making these studies, a distinctive human element, the individuality of persons, has been eliminated as much as possible. That is, we have to eliminate the unique "mineness" which, according to Heidegger, characterizes human existence. It was against the elimination of the individual that Kierkegaard reacted, claiming that what was for the plain man so simple, namely, the unique individual, was for the scholar so complex. One person cannot be substituted for another, and there is no fixed essence that can be assigned to individuals. It is this notion that is captured in the well-known claim that existence precedes essence.

For the existentialist, the individual is aware of and concerned with his possibilities of being and within limits is responsible for the way he is. To put this another way, man has a relation to himself; he can either choose to exist as a distinctive being by realizing his possibilities or he can lose this way of being by becoming so absorbed in the world that everything is decided for him and he becomes just one object among objects.

To exist, writes Macquarrie, "is not simply to 'be,' but is rather to be faced with the choice to 'be or not to be,' to gain existence in the full sense or let it slip away."[4] Talk of existence gaining or losing itself brings to the surface an ambiguity between descriptive and normative use of the word "human." To talk of human existence as gaining or losing itself is not to suggest that persons have the possibility of being nonhuman. It is to state what humans might be. Humans can more fully and less fully realize their potentialities. It is in this context that one can speak of being truly or authentically human, and this suggests that one has in mind some criterion for judging what a truly human life is. Macquarrie suggests that we speak of *becoming* human in the sense that we are discovering and, it is to be hoped, realizing our fullest human potentialities. The criteria, he argues, are to be found within human existence itself. These guidelines are understood to be directions that must be followed if we are to fully realize our potentialities.[5]

Neither Heidegger nor Macquarrie concludes from this emphasis on becoming that no characterizations can be made of human existence. To be sure, one cannot assign fixed essences to the individual, but even the choices of the individual have horizons or limits, and one can discern within these choices certain structures, certain possible ways of being within which the concrete possibilities of any actual person would fall. The task of existential analysis is to describe the universal structures of existence within which concrete choices are made. "Existence," as Macquarrie uses the term, refers to an unfinished kind of being, one open to possibilities that have yet to be realized. The concept of existence shares much in common with the concept of transcending, in which one is said to pass beyond any given stage of one's situation, and with the concept of spirit, which indicates the capacity for creativity and responsibility. Implicit in this notion of existence is a tension between man and nature, for man is in some sense like other entities in the world and at the same time different from them. When the concept of existence is further analyzed, we see, according to Macquarrie, that there are polarities and tensions that in some ways parallel those between existence and nature.

Existentialists have been criticized for talking as if freedom and possibility existed in a vacuum, as if there were no constraints on possible ways of being, and at times this criticism has been deserved. Macquarrie, however, is careful to describe possibilities as existing within certain limits. In this context he draws on Heidegger's language of possibility and facticity. "Facticity" refers to more than factual existence or factual occurrences of some kind of entity. As Heidegger puts it, "The concept of 'facticity' implies that an entity 'within-the-world' has Being-in-the-world in such a way that it can understand itself as bound up in its 'destiny' with the Being of those entities which it encounters within its own world."[6] Man exists in the world not merely in some spatial sense but in the sense of dwelling, of being bound up and occupied with the world. To say that his possibilities exist in tension with his facticity is to say that his possibilities relate to the particular situation in which he finds himself in the world. My possibilities are limited by my facticity, that is, by such givens as intelligence, heredity, environment, and society, and these make up my being in the world. Facticity, writes Macquarrie, "is not an observed state of affairs but the inward, existential awareness of one's own being as a fact that is to be accepted."[7] Heidegger uses "thrownness" as a metaphor to suggest man's factical condition. We become aware of ourselves as having been thrown into a world, having no choice of our race, tradition, intelligence, or finiteness, so that whatever possibilities we have are always set in the framework of facticity. "Existence never escapes from the tension between possibility and facticity. On the one side, man is open and projects his possibilities; on the other side, he is closed by the factical situation in which he already finds himself."[8]

Closely connected with the polarity between possibility and facticity is the polarity between rationality and irrationality, and Macquarrie has referred to the latter tension as the way the former tension is experienced. Rationality, our ability to judge, understand, and interpret, is an important characteristic of what it means to exist. Yet one can hardly ignore the impact of irrationality on one's life, a fact that has been made much of by Freud and others. However much we seek to order our lives and however much reason seems to promise a right ordering of life and unlimited progress, irrationality seems always to be on the verge of threatening to disrupt this progress and order.

A further polarity is suggested by the terms "responsibility" and "impotence." We have already been introduced to the structure of existence in which persons seek to realize their possibilities. Responsibility and impotence point to a more definite moral category of development. The emphasis here is not on obedience to some specific moral principle or to the voice of God but on the actualization of one's own potentialities for being. The term "conscience" is used to refer to that awareness or disclosure of responsibility in which we are summoned, so to speak, to realize our possibilities of being, that is, to free ourselves from determinations from outside ourselves and for self-determination. In Heidegger's language,

> because Dasein is *lost* in the 'they,' it must *find* itself. In order to find *itself* at all, it must be 'shown' to itself in its possible authenticity. In terms of its *possibility,* Dasein *is* already a potentiality-for-Being-its-Self, but it needs to have this potentiality attested . . . we shall claim that this potentiality is attested by that which, in Dasein's everyday interpretation of itself, is familiar to us in the *'voice of conscience'.*[9]

Conscience so defined is the self's awareness of how it measures up to itself. It is a call of the authentic self to the actual self. No universal content can be ascribed to conscience, for within the constraints of existence, each person must realize his own potentiality for being.

Macquarrie is much indebted to Heidegger's discussion of conscience, but he believes that Heidegger, like Nietzsche and Kierkegaard, overemphasizes the role of the individual. Heidegger is correct to avoid losing individual morality in public morality, but he does not, according to Macquarrie, give an adequate account of the redeeming features of collective experience. Although one should allow for individual criticism and creativity in the moral realm, one should not ignore the criticism of individual morality that is exposed by society and other individuals in society. Self-deception is an ever-present possibility in matters of conscience, as is moral weakness in the face of the call of conscience. Heidegger gives little attention to this and to what Luther referred to as bondage and the need for grace. For Macquarrie, the call of conscience is a call to authenticity, a call to a unity of the person, but he argues that this authenticity can be achieved only in affirmative relations with other persons and the material environment. Exploitation of others or of the material environment results in enslavement of the person.

Responsibility refers to the summons to bring order out of disorder, to realize one's own potentiality for being in relation to the world and others. Macquarrie argues that the summons to responsibility always stands in tension with impotence, with the failure to achieve what we are summoned to achieve. The polarities of existence described thus far may seem to suggest an absurdity or meaninglessness in existence. Being torn between possibility, rationality, and responsibility on the one hand and facticity, irrationality, and impotence on the other, with the understanding that existence always looks toward death, suggests, as Sartre put it, that life is not meaningful and that man is a useless passion. Yet, we seem to go on living as if life is not ultimately meaningless. This suggests another polarity in existence, anxiety and hope, which, according to Macquarrie, sums up all the others.

Given the polarities of existence, man is never free from anxiety, never free from "a sense of the threat of absurdity and negativity."[10] Yet there is, however, also hope that existence is somehow worthwhile. In *Being and Time,* Heidegger focuses on the moods of anxiety and fear but does not analyze hope. It is possible to argue, however, that even his analysis does not result in a hopeless and nihilistic view of existence, that hope is at least implicit in his analysis.

Although Heidegger's analysis of anxiety differs from that of Kierkegaard, who treated the concepts of anxiety and sin in conjunction, Heidegger did say that Kierkegaard had gone further than anyone in analyzing the concept. Heidegger himself analyzes anxiety in the context of his understanding of "falling," which has some affinities with the Biblical notion of sin. According to Heidegger, anxiety is a mood that discloses our existence in the face of its limits, its nothingness, the possibility that it might not be. But as anxiety stretches Dasein out into its nothingness, it also brings one back from absorption in the world of everyday concerns and confronts existence with responsibility for itself. "Anxiety makes manifest in Dasein its *Being-towards* its ownmost potentiality-for-Being—that is, its *Being-free for* the freedom of choosing itself and taking hold of itself. Anxiety brings Dasein face to face with its *Being-free for (propensio in . . .)* the authenticity of its Being, and for this authenticity as a possibility, which it always is."[11] Anxiety confronts us with the possibility of our nothingness, but to the extent that it also discloses our potentiality, it is not merely threatening. The more positive dimension implicit in Heidegger's analysis of anxiety is brought out forcefully in Macquarrie's analysis of hope.

To talk of realizing or choosing our potentiality for Being is in some sense to talk of the future, to trust in the future, to hope. Macquarrie writes: "Wherever people work to produce something, wherever they cultivate the fields, wherever they marry, wherever they found and raise families, wherever they learn or teach, wherever they engage in political activities, there is hope. For in all these activities and in a host of others that have not been mentioned, there is an affirmation of the future, a trust in the future, an investment in the future."[12] Without hope, without trust that the future presents us with an open texture for development, there would be no point in talking of our potentiality for authenticity, for being other than we are.

This does not mean that hope must ignore the limits imposed on growth and development or the forces that work against the fulfillment of our potentiality for existing authentically in relation to the world and others. Hope, unlike naive optimism, or what we might call irrational belief in progress, need not ignore the evils and ambiguities of existing in the world. Says Macquarrie: "In contrast to all the optimisms that proclaim themselves, true hope lives in the awareness of the world's evils, sufferings, and lacks. Hope must remain vulnerable to evidence that counts against it. . . ."[13]

According to Macquarrie, the poles of anxiety and hope are not contradictory. When understood in relation to each other, they present us with a realistic understanding of ourselves. On the one hand, we are limited by what threatens our way of being in the world, and on the other we are open to choosing our fullest potentiality for being in the world. Anxiety and hope are challenges both to sheer absurdity and meaninglessness and to irrational optimism. To the extent that they disclose our being in the world, anxiety and hope are also not merely subjective experiences. Expressions they give rise to may be evaluated as adequately or inadequately disclosing the character of our being in the world.[14]

Macquarrie's analysis thus far has emphasized the individual and the disclosure of his potentialities for being. The individual, however, always exists in relation to others, and that suggests another polarity in human existence, between the individual and society. Even Sartre, who emphasizes the individual and the negative impact of human relations on the individual in *Being and Nothingness*, speaks of the possibility of mediated reciprocity. And Heidegger, who also makes the individual primary considers being-with-others to be a structure of Dasein equi-primordial with Being-in-the-world.[15] Such existentialists as Jaspers, Marcel, and Buber go even further in analyzing the social character of existence and human community. The interdependence of persons is fundamental to their thought.

From his earliest work, Macquarrie has expressed dissatisfaction with Heidegger's and Bultmann's understanding of human existence, arguing that they have not adequately taken the social aspects into account. Human sexuality, family, language, and the economic life of man are only a few factors that suggest the interdependence of human beings and their need for community. These are, according to Macquarrie, manifestations of a fundamental need to go beyond oneself, to transcend toward others. Yet this drive toward others comes up against the uniqueness of the individual. Each individual is in some sense unique and unrepeatable and looks at the world from within a framework that is ultimately impenetrable, even by a close friend or loved one. There is, in other words, a polarity within existence between our need for human community and our need for individuality and privacy. This polarity historically manifests itself in societies that oppress individuals and in self-seeking individuals who disrupt communities. The extremes of privacy and dependence are both expressions of unfulfilled potentialities for being in the world in relation to other persons and things.

It has been suggested that there is always the possibility that existence is an absurdity, a way of being for which there is no meaning, and when we turn to the actual human condition, we are often struck by the disorder and imbalance between the poles of the various polarities of existence. The tension between poles is not maintained. Descriptions of the actual human condition are infinite, says Macquarrie, but there are two primary categories for understanding the disorders of actual existence. The first category includes such disorders as pride, tyranny, angelism, utopianism, and individualism. These disorders arise from a refusal to give proper recognition to our facticity and finiteness, the limitations of human existence, and from the desire to enjoy a superhuman existence free from all the restraints that help make up our existence in the world. The second category includes such disorders as sensual indulgence, insensitivity to others, despair, and the irresponsibility of collectivism. These disorders are said to be founded on man's retreat from possibility, responsibility, and even rationality. Here Macquarrie refers to that mode of existence in which persons try to live in and for the present.

The first category of disorder is said to have been particularly manifest in the great tyrants of history, although to a lesser degree its forms may be in all of us. The second category of disorder is more characteristic of the masses. Macquarrie would concede that at times the disorders of existence have been exaggerated to totally characterize all of human existence. But he believes that one should not underestimate their importance in analyzing human existence or fail to recognize their universality. Few would deny the reality of such imbalances in human exis-

tence, and many who talk of alienation and narcissism are referring to similar disorders even when their interpretations differ.

The fundamental disorder, argues Macquarrie, is an alienation from oneself, a falling-away from the full range of one's
possibility and facticity. But this self-alienation also leads to an
alienation between persons, with radical individualism at one
extreme and radical collectivism at the other. Ultimately, suggests Macquarrie, alienation may even lead to a sense of lostness
in which one feels cut off not only from his place in the scheme of
things but from reality itself. Alienation in this extreme sense is
being unable to find any kinship in the surrounding world.
Human life becomes totally isolated from all that surrounds it. In
this context, the religious person uses the word "sin" to point
ultimately to a separation from Being or God. Macquarrie is not,
of course, claiming that all persons would acknowledge alienation in the wider sense. He is claiming that the recognition of this
alienation from Being is a possibility for all and that the theological understanding of alienation is grounded in a widely recognized element of man's understanding of himself in the world.[16]

The late nineteenth and early twentieth centuries were char-
acterized by a widespread optimistic belief that the sciences and
education could overcome the disorders of human existence. But
as Jaspers has said, this belief was shattered in August 1914. Since
then we have been much more sensitive to the seeming intrac-
tability of many of our human problems. "Alienation" has replaced "progress" as the catchword of our time. This suggests to
Macquarrie that our options are considerably sharpened, so that
"either we acknowledge the absurdity of a situation in which we
find ourselves responsible for an existence which we lack the
capacity to master, and have just to make the best of a bad job; or
else we look for a further dimension in the situation, a depth
beyond both man and nature that is open to us in such a way that
it can make sense of our finite existence by supporting it and
bringing order and fulfillment to it."[17]

Many would certainly argue that making do with what we
have is all that is necessary, and Macquarrie would grant that
there is no necessary connection between the recognition of
widespread disorder in existence and a search for support from
beyond human existence. Nevertheless, Macquarrie has pro-

vided a frame of reference in which this search can be understood. This is the point at which, in contrast to Sartre, Heidegger talks of the grace of Being and Jaspers talks of a kind of immanent grace within human existence. Macquarrie would agree that not all those who reject the need for support from beyond human existence need turn to the kind of pessimism suggested by Sartre, particularly in his early work. He also recognizes that merely pointing to this alternative is not sufficient to establish that there is any reason to believe in some source from beyond man that could enable him to overcome the disorders of existence. Macquarrie does believe, however, that his analysis can help show that human experience itself makes sense of the search for meaning and the idea of grace of which religious persons speak.

For Macquarrie, grace is understood in the context of seeking to make sense of and bring order to human existence in its being in the world. "Authentic existence" is the term used to designate this ordered self. In the English translation of Heidegger's *Being and Time,* the term *eigentlich* is translated as "authentic" and means "ownness" or "mineness." Macquarrie describes authentic selfhood, however, as possible only within a community of selves in which the polarities of community and individuality are held in tension.

Much talk about self and selfhood in Western thought is rooted in the dualism of ancient Greek thought, particularly Plato. For Plato, the soul is immortal, having existed prior to its union with body and continuing to exist after the end of the existence of the body. Dualism became even more explicit in Descartes' two-substance theory of mind and body and has been carried over into contemporary thought in the debate between materialists and immaterialists. Although few philosophers today would describe themselves as strict dualists, this way of talking of the self stands in the background of many contemporary discussions about whether everything essential about the self can be said in material or behavioral terms. Much of the history of Western religious thought concerning the self has also been dominated by a dualism between mind and body or soul and body. The soul is often conceived to be a separate substance providing unity, stability, and in some cases immortality for the self. When the unity and stability of the self are talked about in this way, there seems little difference between the unity and stability associated with persons and those associated with rocks. In both cases the emphasis seems to be on its persistence through time. The difference between time as a series of nows and temporality or the experience of time is, as we shall see, important to Macquarrie's understanding of human existence and Being.

Many contemporary thinkers dispute the notion of a substantial soul. It has been argued in a variety of ways that we are what we are precisely in our being in the world in relation to persons and things and that when queried, the disembodied soul seems to disappear into what Gilbert Ryle called the ghost in the machine. Macquarrie agrees with those who think that the idea of a ghostly soul inhabiting a body is confusing and superfluous. He agrees with the existentialists that the traditional dualistic model of selfhood is a reductionist model in which substance is held to be a solid, enduring object like that of a rock. Macquarrie and Heidegger argue that this model ignores what is distinctive about persons, what sets them apart from other entities. The self, says Macquarrie, "has a dynamism, a complexity, a diversity-in-unity, that can never be expressed in terms of inert thinghood, even if we refine this conception as far as we can and dignify it with the notion of 'substantiality.'"[18]

Descartes' use of the word *res* in speaking of *res cogitans* and *res extensa,* Macquarrie argues, suggests that Descartes conceived of both mind and body as analogous to a thing, a solid, enduring object. Macquarrie rejects this dualistic understanding of the self, but he does not opt for a reduction of the self to what can be expressed in physicalistic or behavioristic terms. Certain aspects of selfhood cannot be contained within reductionist explanations. As freedom is the presupposition of our responsible activities, Macquarrie argues, so the "I," or the ego, must be a presupposition of the self. Ego in this sense, however, cannot be objectified without turning it into something that it is not. There is a self-awareness that comes before objectification; Sartre calls this the pre-reflective ego. The 'I,' or the ego, is in this sense the precondition for any reflection on the self as object. It is the subject's awareness of himself as a subject, as thinking, and as initiating action.[19]

Macquarrie admits that this pre-reflective ego cannot be empirically demonstrated, but he believes this to be an objection only if we are seeking to understand the self as analogous to a material thing or a biological organism. Like John Macmurray, Macquarrie sees an important place for empirical studies of human nature, but also like Macmurray, he argues that in fully understanding human existence, we must employ fully personal categories. These categories are held to be *sui generis* and irreducible. Macquarrie places great emphasis on what we might call the "spirituality" of man, on his self-consciousness, freedom, and transcendence as corrective to materialistic and behavioristic explanations. He also recognizes that the spirituality of man can be exaggerated so that the materiality of man is forgotten. Macquarrie agrees with Ryle that one should not speak as if the self were a ghostly inhabitor of a body, and he argues that the self is somehow "embodied." In speaking of the self's embodiment, Macquarrie appropriates the language of Aristotle, who talks of the soul as the form of the body, the *hegemonikon* that gives direction to the body. As Chapter 3 will explain, Macquarrie interprets the Aristotelian view in a dynamic sense, in keeping with his understanding of the Heideggerian view of the relation between Being and beings. The bodily and the spiritual are not reducible to each other, but they are unified in persons, albeit to greater or lesser degrees. In a manner reminiscent of Strawson, Macquarrie speaks of "person" as an irreducible category and a single reality to which may be attributed bodily and spiritual characteristics. Ultimately, however, given the dynamic notion with which he is operating, this unity is understood to be a potentiality, something to be achieved amid the conflicting tendencies within a person.[20]

Heidegger, on whom Macquarrie is primarily dependent for his conception of selfhood, also rejects the dualism of Plato and the tendency to speak of the self in terms of the model of thinghood, and his view has much in common with Aristotle and with the Biblical notion of self. For Heidegger and Macquarrie, *temporality,* not thinghood, is the proper model for understanding the self. As possibility, the self is directed toward the future. Selfhood is not something given, as the Platonic notion of soul suggests, but is something to be achieved or lost in the realization or failure to realize one's potentialities. In the language of Aristotle, the self or soul is the entelechy of the body, the bringing to fulfillment of the potentialities of embodied existence in the world. As we have seen, for Heidegger and Macquarrie, possibility exists in tension with facticity, with its heritage of what has been. Self exists in the present between its possibility (future) and its past (facticity).

When the model of temporality is used in talking about the self, human existence is clearly distinguished from other existing things and the unity of the self is understood differently from the way we understand the unity of inanimate objects. A rock may have a past, present, and future in the sense that it endures through a series of nows, but its unity differs from that of a persons', whose self takes time into itself, gathering past, present, and future into the moment of personal existence. It would make no sense, for example, to talk of a rock being at odds with itself, losing itself, or realizing itself. Yet this is the way we often speak of persons. The disorders of existence Macquarrie has described can be best understood as an imbalance between the temporal dimensions of existence. Irresponsibility, for example, can be understood as a manifestation of dwelling in the past and ignoring responsibility for the future. Utopianism can be understood as living in the future and ignoring one's facticity, one's heritage from the past.

Emphasis on the self as thinking subject reached its fullest expression in the idealists. If the model of temporality is adopted for understanding the self, however, the emphasis is on the self as agent, to use the expression of John Macmurray. This emphasis in no way rejects the role of self as thinking subject. It suggests instead that selfhood is manifest most fully and most typically in what Heidegger calls resoluteness and what others call willing. Whether existence is held to be autonomous, making the best of one's own resources, or is believed to look beyond itself for fulfillment, there is widespread agreement among the existentialists that at the center of human existence there is an act of will that pulls the self together.

In distinguishing between authentic and inauthentic modes of existence, Heidegger uses the terms "resoluteness" and "irresoluteness." "Irresoluteness" characterizes existence as dwelling in the present, as enduring from one now to another. As such, human existence differs little from other entities. It is no longer in control of its selfhood. In irresolute, or inauthentic existence, the self displays no will of its own, no realization of its possibilities; it is carried from moment to moment by outside determinants. Irresoluteness is a living in the present and a forgetting of one's possibilities. In Heidegger's language,

> Dasein has *forgotten* itself in its ownmost *thrown* poten-tiality-for-Being. This forgetting is not nothing, nor is it just a failure to remember; it is rather a 'positive' ecstat-ical mode of one's having been, a mode with a character of its own. The ecstasis (rapture) of forgetting has the character of backing away *in the face of* one's ownmost 'been,' and of doing so in a manner which is closed off from itself—in such a manner, indeed, that his backing away closes off ecstatically that in the face of which one is backing away, and thereby closes itself off too.[21]

In contrast, "resoluteness" and "authentic existence" refer to that mode of existence in which Dasein gains control of its way of being and holds together the ecstasies of past, present and future.

> For the temporality of resoluteness has, with relation to its Present, the character of a *moment of vision*. When such a moment makes the Situation authentically present, this making-present does not itself take the lead, but is *held* in that future which is in the process of having-been. One's existence in the moment of vision temporalizes itself as something that has been stretched along in a way which is fatefully whole in the sense of the authentic historical *constancy* of the Self.[22]

The moment of vision to which Heidegger refers is the authentic moment, the moment in which the three dimensions of the temporality of human existence are disclosed in their unity.

Commitment, understood within the accepted limits of facticity, is what gives shape and direction to our life through the development of stable conditions and policies of action. Macquarrie's *In Search of Humanity* describes three essential char-acteristics of commitment. First, commitment relates to the task of forming a self or becoming a person. In our commitment to vocation, friendship, and marriage, for example, we are said to develop our character, without which we would in some merely passive way conform to our environment. Second, commitment relates to our self-transcendence, to our going beyond our self as isolated from the world and others. Through our commitment we become related to the world and the society in which we live and perhaps ultimately to the wider range of Being or God. Third, commitment involves self-limitation. We become what we are within our limits of time, wisdom, and resources, and every commitment of depth is at the same time a renunciation because to commit oneself in one direction is to divert oneself from other directions. Existence in the absence of commitment would be a life without direction, a drifting from moment to moment.[23]

Commitment should always be understood in the context of accepting our facticity, our limits. Acceptance of our being-toward-death is held to be essential to the full realization of our possibilities. The possibility of death plays an important role in the achievement of authentic selfhood, as Macquarrie makes clear, and also helps us to understand the role of religious faith in human experience. It is no accident that at a time when many have become disillusioned with the notion of progress in society, courses in death and dying are multiplying on university campuses. Indeed, unrestricted emphasis on progress and optimism might be said to cover over a deeper sense of pessimism, one which seeks to avoid our facticity by escaping from it. Death, perhaps more than any other possibility of our being in the world, brings us up against our limits and threatens to close off the future. Death exposes the superficiality of many of our aspirations and confronts us in a radical way with our finiteness, our limitedness. It is our being-toward-death which raises the fundamental question of what it means to be.

Heidegger's analysis of death occurs in the context of his asking whether we can grasp Dasein's being as a whole. Since Dasein is always possibility, it is always projecting ahead of itself; there is always something to be settled, something outstanding in one's potentiality for being. This suggests that as long as Dasein is an entity, it never reaches its wholeness, and when nothing more is outstanding, it is already annihilated, no longer being in the world. "When Dasein reaches its wholeness in death, it simultaneously loses the Being of its 'there.' By its transition to no-longer-Dasein, it gets lifted right out of the possibility of experiencing this transition and of understanding itself as something experienced."[24] Awareness of death does not suggest for Heidegger that existence is absurd or meaningless. In anticipation of death, Dasein is understood to be wrenched away from the crowd; its own being becomes an issue. To anticipate death is to face up to the limit of one's existence and gather up the possibilities of existence in a unity between birth and death.

Macquarrie argues that Heidegger's analysis of death provides us with important insights into the nature of human existence and points beyond any mere nihilistic interpretation on at least two accounts. First, the possibility of death is understood to be integrative rather than destructive of human existence. To exist authentically is in part to live in anticipation of one's death. This puts into perspective the superficiality and triviality of many ambitions and aspirations. As Macquarrie argues:

> In such an existence as a being-towards-death, the anticipation of death plays something like the part which the eschatological expectation played in primitive Christianity, and perhaps Heidegger is no more a nihilist than was St. Paul. Both see human existence as lying before the imminent end, in the face of which responsible decisions have to be made, and in the light of which all the possibilities that lie before the end have to be evaluated.[25]

Second, Heidegger's understanding of anxiety in the face of death has the positive character of calling man from the forgetfulness of Being. In *Being And Time,* Being-toward-death is understood to include an awareness of what it means not to be and hence an awareness of what it means to be. In "What Is Metaphysics?" (1928), Heidegger focuses on the experience of not-being, in relation to which beings are understood as beings, and not-being or Nothing is disclosed as an essential aspect of Being. This, as Macquarrie suggests, prepares the way for Heidegger's so-called meditative thinking of Being. A parallel to this experience in Christian theology is suggested in the work of Paul Tillich, who speaks of the shock of non-being as a prelude to the revelatory experience.[26]

Macquarrie does not overstate the parallel between Heidegger's description of the experience of non-being and Christian theology, but he suggests that Heidegger's analysis of death in connection with the achievement of authentic selfhood may help one to undertand the possibility of religious faith. The possibility of being-toward-death, for both Heidegger and Macquarrie, provides an awareness of the limits to human existence and a focus for the ordering of existence. Selfhood, according to Macquarrie, can only be achieved when we look beyond the superficial and take our finitude and mortality up into our potentiality, which projects us into the future. Death suggests the futility of many of our transient concerns, and the confrontation with this possibility may lead us to seek meaning in the situation in which the being that we are is understood to be part and parcel of the being that we can be. For some persons, the possibility of death suggests that all human aspirations are pointless, but the person of religious faith sees the polarities of his beginning and end within the wider context of Being. Faith, according to Macquarrie, is an existential attitude in which man looks beyond himself and reliance on his own resources to the wider range of Being within which man's being finds its understanding and support.

Faith, in the sense that Macquarrie speaks of it here, is not belief in some set of propositions, although beliefs are implicit in faith. Faith is an understanding of the self in relation to Being, an understanding born in an attitude of acceptance and commitment. It is here that the difference between the religious and the non-religious person can be seen. "Religious faith, as faith in being, looks to the wider being within which our existence is set for support; it discovers a meaning for existence that is already given with existence: the alternative attitude looks for no support from beyond man, who must rely on his own resources and who must himself create for his life any meaning that it can have."[27] Macquarrie does not mean to suggest that only men of religious faith can take a hopeful attitude toward human existence. Even Sartre did not wallow in the absurdity of existence. Nor does he mean to suggest that the person of faith is ever anchored complacently in his hopefulness. Faith itself is an attitude that is subject to continual testing and renewal. It is a part of our finiteness that neither the man of faith nor the man of unfaith will gain certitude. To gain such certitude would require that we step outside our existence, outside our historicity. Yet in the absence of certitude, we are faced with deciding how we will understand and make sense of our existence, and Macquarrie believes the limiting cases to be religious faith at one extreme and a kind of Sartrean acceptance of absurdity at the other.[28]

Our treatment of Macquarrie's analysis of existence and Being has avoided the question of the justification of faith. We have presented the attitude of faith as an option consistent with an analysis of the structures of human existence, an attitude that arises out of the search for a meaningful existence. The procedure Macquarrie follows is to describe the essential characteristics of the Being of human existence, inviting readers to see if they recognize their own existence in this description. By drawing attention to the disorders of existence, Macquarrie hopes to show the inadequacy of the view of man as self-sufficient so that we might become open to an understanding of the wider context of Being in which the person of religious faith discovers the meaningfulness of his existence. We now turn to Macquarrie's account of the content of this faith.

Notes

1. Martin Heidegger, *Being and Time*, translated by John Macquarrie and Edward Robinson (New York: Harper and Row, 1962), p. 58.
2. *Being and Time*, p. 67.
3. *Being and Time*, p. 67.
4. Macquarrie, *Existentialism* (London: Hutchinson, 1972), p. 54.
5. Macquarrie, *In Search of Humanity*, (London: SCM Press, 1982), Chapter I. On this basis Macquarrie also argues for a reconstruction of natural law. See *Three Issues in Ethics* (London: SCM Press, 1970).
6. *Being and Time*, p. 82.
7. *Existentialism*, p. 148.
8. *Existentialism*, pp. 149–50.
9. *Being and Time*, p. 313.
10. *Principles*, p. 64.
11. *Being and Time*, p. 232.
12. Macquarrie, *Christian Hope* (New York: Seabury, 1978), p. 4.
13. *Christian Hope*, p. 13.
14. *Studies*, pp. 31–42.
15. *Being and Time*, pp. 149ff.
16. *Principles*, p. 71. *In Search of Humanity*, pp. 107–24.
17. *Principles*, p. 73.
18. *Principles*, p. 75.
19. *In Search of Humanity*, pp. 38–42. For Macquarrie's alternative to doctrines of the immortality of the soul and the resurrection of the body, see *Christian Hope*, pp. 112ff.
20. *In Search of Humanity*, pp. 47–58.
21. *Being and Time*, pp. 388–89.
22. *Being and Time*, p. 463.
23. *In Search of Humanity*, pp. 142–45.
24. *Being and Time*, p. 281.
25. *Studies*, pp. 56–57.
26. *Studies*, p. 57.
27. *Principles*, p. 80.
28. *Principles*, pp. 80–81.

3

BEING
AND
GOD

THE WORD "GOD" IS USED IN A VARIETY OF CONTEXTS TO SIGNIFY at one pole transcendent Being and at the other some transcendent dimension of human experience. The two poles are not accidental in efforts to speak adequately of God. One has to account for the belief in a reality that is other than the finite entities which make up the world as we know it and without which such entities would not be. One also has to account for the religious understanding of reality in which God is believed to be intrinsically related to the meanings and purposes of human existence. During the first half of the twentieth century, theologians tended to stress the infinite qualitative difference between God and world in contrast to the more immanental tendencies of the nineteenth-century theologians, with the result that God was thought of primarily as a transcendent, self-sufficient Being set over against the world. More recently, under the influence of such philosophers as Whitehead, Hartshorne, and Heidegger theologians have developed a more organic view of the relation between world and God. Macquarrie shares much with classical theists, yet he argues that we have passed beyond the God of classical theism, that is,

(37)

beyond the idea of God as a personal being, albeit invisible, bodiless, and intangible, who created the world, exercises governance over it, and intervenes on occasions. The need for positing such a God has diminished, he argues, as the scientific capacity to account for the events of the world has grown. Macquarrie has not yet provided a fully developed theory of God to replace the God of classical theism; but he has taken several significant steps in that direction, as we shall see.

Philosophers frequently make a distinction between belief-in and belief-that and theologians have made a similar distinction in speaking of faith and belief. To say that I believe in or have faith in, is to say that I am committed to or that I trust. For example, I might say that I believe in a friend, a country, or a classical education. But belief-in also involves belief-that. It would be strange, for instance, for me to believe in a friend without believing in some sense that he is real and that he is trustworthy. In a similar way, Macquarrie argues that religious faith involves some kind of ontological commitment and that human existence is fulfilled only in communion with a reality that transcends its existence. He disagrees with those who reduce talk of God to talk of a meeting or encounter and argues that one cannot avoid the question of ontological commitment. Bultmann may be correct in emphasizing that religious faith is more than believing in an idea of God, but Macquarrie believes he errs in failing to provide a satisfactory account of the God of whom he speaks.

Belief in God, according to Macquarrie, means "faith in Being," and he adds, "By this I understand an attitude of acceptance and commitment in the face not only of my own being or even that of the society in which I find myself, but ultimately of that wider being within which human society and history have themselves their setting."[1] Macquarrie also says that faith in Being can be understood to mean that "reality is trustworthy at the deepest level" and suggests that Schubert Ogden is saying something similar when he declares that "the primary use or function of the word 'God' is to refer to the objective ground in reality itself of our ineradicable confidence in the final worth of our existence."[2]

Macquarrie does not hold that religious faith entails belief in the existence of a supernatural being beyond the world. Yet he rejects accounts of religious faith which either would do away with a need for the word "God" or have it refer only to some dimension of human experience. How then are we to understand the referent of the word "God" if faith in God is taken to mean "faith in Being" or "reality is trustworthy"? Macquarrie would answer by saying that God is Being or Holy Being. With the phrase "Holy Being" he is emphasizing that God is both the highest reality and the highest value. On the one hand, God is the supreme value, what Tillich called the object of ultimate concern. On the other hand, God is understood to explain, to provide intelligibility, to answer the question why things are rather than are not. And it is because of this that Macquarrie refers to God as the highest reality as well as the highest value. God is both *ens realissimum* and *summum bonum,* and both can be conceived of in the concept of God as *esse,* as act of Being.[3] Macquarrie understands this to be a biblical notion expressed in Hebrews 11:16. God is the supreme reality (he is) and he is the supreme good (he rewards those who seek him).

This is not, of course, the first time that "God" has been equated with "Being." But in relating the two terms, Macquarrie is appealing specifically to the Heideggerian concept of Being. Being, according to Heidegger, is not an entity. It is that without which beings would not be and as such cannot itself be a being. It is no-thing from the standpoint of existing entities. Heidegger argues that traditional modes of thinking were directed toward entities and thus Being was thought of as if it were an entity, albeit the greatest entity. This failure to think of Being as Being, according to Heidegger, has resulted in the forgetfulness of Being in the tradition of Western metaphysics. Although Heidegger does not equate Being with God, Macquarrie claims that we can legitimately make this connection on the grounds that Western theology has also participated in the forgetfulness of Being, with the result that God has been inadequately thought of as an entity.

In treating "God" as synonymous with "Being," Macquarrie is in one sense aligning himself with the classical theological tradition. He notes, for example, the long association of the idea of God with the idea of Being in the Greek Fathers, St. Augustine, and St. Thomas and suggests that if one conceives of God as immeasurably the greatest being and as different from particular beings altogether, one is moving toward the thought of

God as Being, albeit in an ambiguous way.[4] This ambiguity partly accounts for the idea of God as a personal being set over against the world, one who created the world, exercises governance over it, and intervenes on occasions. It is this notion of God which Macquarrie claims to have passed beyond. The root of Macquarrie's break with classical theism, then, is to be found in the unambiguous claim that God is not a being but Being itself. This, however, is a fundamental shift in the way of conceiving of God and one which rejects the traditional dualistic conception of the relation between God and world.

If we are to understand Macquarrie's conception of God and his understanding of the relation between God and world, we need to develop further his understanding of Being. Macquarrie cites Heidegger in referring to Being as "the *transcendens* pure and simple."[5] Being is already thought with every entity and is the condition that there are entities at all. Being is not merely the class of things, nor is it a property of things, and in the strict sense, as we have said, it is not something that is. As the condition for the being of all particular entities, Being cannot itself be an entity. Nor, says Macquarrie, can Being be understood according to any model of thinghood. Being is not a mere substance; it is the act by which things are rather than are not. But this does not, according to Macquarrie, imply a lack of stability or identity in Being. To say that Being is a dynamic process, or that which enables beings, is to say that becoming is both distinct from and included in Being. Apart from becoming, Being would remain pure undifferentiated nothing, the "dark night in which all cows are black," as Hegel says in the *Phenomenology of Spirit*. Yet Being cannnot be fully interpreted in terms of becoming, for becoming is unintelligible apart from some conception of Being in which becoming is included. Mere becoming or flux is chaos.[6]

In talking of Being or God in this dynamic sense, Macquarrie is primarily influenced by Heidegger, who signifies this dynamism by using a verbal noun, *Sein,* in his talk of Being. But Macquarrie recognizes that Heidegger is not the only contemporary thinker to break with the traditional way of talking about God or Being in terms of substance. On the contrary, he sees something of a consensus emerging on this point between such diverse thinkers as Heidegger and Jaspers, Whitehead and Hartshorne, and Marechal and Teilhard.[7] Macquarrie also finds

Biblical support for this way of talking about God. Referring to Exodus 3:14, where God makes known his name to Moses, saying, "I am who I am," Macquarrie argues that the verb "to be" includes within it the notion "to become" and that the passage might be better translated as, "I let be what I let be." God not only is but is in a dynamic and creative sense. Thus, says Macquarrie, God might be better described as He Who Lets Be rather than He Who Is.[8]

For Macquarrie, Being is not a property or a class or the sum of beings.

> Being is rather a *transcendens* which, as above all catego-
> ries, must remain mysterious, and yet is not just a blank
> incomprehensible. The very fact that it is the condition
> that there may be any beings or properties of beings is an
> indication that although we cannot say of being that it
> 'is,' and might even say that it is 'nothing that is,' being
> 'is' nevertheless more beingful than anything that is, for it
> is the prior condition that anything may be.[9]

Being is the act that enables things to be or, as Macquarrie prefers to say, Being is letting-be. Using that term, Macquarrie is stressing the dynamic sense of Being, the sense that might be partially grasped in such terms as "energy" or "act." The words "letting-be" express the creative relation between Being and beings in that letting-be is prior to particular instances of being. It is clear that by "letting-be" Macquarrie does not mean leaving alone or not interfering. He means enabling to be or empowering or bringing into being. Yeow Choo Lak has expressed the point concisely: "A being *is* in virtue of the fact that it is, but Being is not something that is but lets-be and therefore precedes any is-ness. So, Being is different from beings, yet it is the *spring* and *origin* of all beings; the beings are contingent on and originate from Being."[10]

This concept of Being as letting-be can be further understood through the notions of presence and manifestation. Being is the *transcendens,* the incomparable, and would remain nothing apart from its appearances in and through particular beings. Being, as that which enables being to be, is not a thing in itself behind its appearances but gives itself in and through its appearances. As such, Being which is furthest from us is also closest to us in its presence in every being, including our own. Presumably, any being may become a manifestation of Being, but Being is said to be grasped with least distortion in those entities that display the widest range of what it means to be, and here personal being has a particular role to play.[11]

Macquarrie is attempting in this notion of letting-be to capture the meaning of two models used in talking about Being or God as Creator. The dominant model is that of "making," as in "God made the firmament." This model has the advantage of stressing the transcendence of God as one who makes the world. But it has the disadvantage of suggesting a dualistic relation between one being and another. It suggests the image of a factory worker making an article for our use. The model of maker needs to be supplemented by the model of emanation, in which we think of the sun sending forth its rays. This model suggests the immanence of Being in creation. The relation between God as Creator and the world is closer to that between an artist and his painting than it is to the relation between the factory worker and the object of production. The artist has, in a sense, put himself into his creation, and although the painting has a life of its own, there is a sense in which the painting is an extension of the artist himself. He is in the painting just as the painting has been in him. In talking of Being or God as letting-be, Macquarrie is trying to express the idea of Being as the *transcendens* which, in its letting-be, is immanent and manifest in all particular entities and on which all entities are dependent.

In summary, we may say that for Macquarrie Being is not an entity. It is the *transcendens,* the incomparable that enables or lets beings be and is present and manifest in them. It is clear that Macquarrie intends that this way of talking about Being also apply to God. "Our final analysis of being as the *incomparable* that *lets-be* and is *present-and-manifest* is strikingly parallel to the analysis of the numinous as *mysterium trememendum et fascinans.*"[12] This association between "Being" and "God," however creates some difficulties. H. P. Owen, for instance, claims that Macquarrie's application of "letting-be" to Being is ontologically illicit because only God can "let-be."[13] We need, then, to look more closely at the relation between "God" and "Being" and at Macquarrie's distinction between them.

Macquarrie claims that the words are not synonyms, that "Being" is a neutral designator and that "God" carries with it an existential connotation of valuation and worship, so that "God" is synonymous with "Holy Being." Two issues here need to be clarified. First, when Macquarrie refers to "Being" as a neutral designator, he is acknowledging that "Being" is not always understood as a synonym for "God." Sartre, for example, uses the word "Being" but does not equate it with God, and religious believers would not equate the idea of God with Sartre's idea of Being as absurd or alien. Second, Macquarrie does not intend to suggest that talk of God as Holy Being rather than Being is the result merely of a change of attitude. The whole thrust of Macquarrie's and, for that matter, Heidegger's talk of Being concerns experiences and reflections that make us aware of the disclosure of Being in itself and from itself. Macquarrie would agree with Owen that an analysis of finite beings does not lead by logical necessity to the idea of God. But he would want to argue that describing Being as holy provides a more adequate account of the experience of existence and Being than alternative accounts and also provides some justification for the religious person's commitment to Being understood as gracious.

This understanding of God as Being or Holy Being makes Macquarrie reluctant to use the word "exists" with reference to God. Macquarrie argues that the real issue between atheists and theists is not about the existence of God but about the understanding of Being as alien or gracious. "Exists" is an exceedingly complex word and we use it in a variety of contexts. We may talk, for example, of the existence of mathematical ideas, tables, electrons, and people. Henceforth in this chapter this general use of the word will be called "exists$_1$." One might refer to it as an ontic sense of "exists," one most clearly expressed in such sentences as "There exists an instance of X." The intent in such sentences is not to describe the entity referred to but to indicate that it is. "Exists" in this sense does not appear to have one determinate sense; rather it is dependent on the context in which the word is used, and the conditions under which we are prepared to say that ideas, tables, electrons, and people exist will vary. Nevertheless, those things that are said to exist may be said to make up the totality of what exists.

A second use of the word "exists" which we shall call

"exists₂", is commonly understood by the existentialist to indicate the kind of existence that pertains to humans. "Existence" in this case indicates something about the character or nature of man. As we saw in Chapter 2, when Heidegger says that "the essence of Dasein lies in its existence," he means that Dasein is constituted by its possible ways of being. Milton Munitz speaks in a related way about the way the world exists. He is not defining "exists" in the existentialist's specialized sense. Nor is he denying the legitimacy of using "exists" in sentences like "There exists an instance of X." He is pointing out that "exists" is a verb that has a descriptive use with reference to the world. "Exists" in this sense refers to some form of activity and, as applied to the world, is said to designate "what the world does."[14] Both Munitz and the existentialists use the term in a descriptive sense.

Although Macquarrie may occasionally blur the distinction between what we have called exists₁ and exists₂, it is clear that he is aware of a variety of ways that "exists" is used, as well as of the general distinction we have made. In *Principles of Christian Theology*, he cites both the existentialist and the "traditional" uses of "exists" and indicates a reluctance to use either with reference to God. Speaking of the existentialist use of "exists," he writes, "If we use the word in this specialized sense, then we cannot say that God exists, just as we cannot say that a river exists, or a horse, or an angel. But this has nothing to do with the question of the 'reality' of any of them." Macquarrie goes on to indicate that "exists" has been traditionally used in a much wider sense (perhaps we should say a different sense) "to mean anything that has being," and it is in this sense, he says, that one has traditionally argued for or against the existence of God. Again, Macquarrie is reluctant to say "God exists." He writes: "Strictly speaking, however, one cannot say that God exists in this way either, for if God is being and not *a* being, then one can say no more that God *is* than being *is*. God (or being) *is* not, but rather *lets be*."[15]

Thus far, Macquarrie's position seems fairly straightforward. One cannot apply "exists" in the existentialist sense to God because that sense is restricted to human existence, and one cannot apply "exists" in the traditional sense to God because such existence can be predicated only of beings. God is not a being, but Being itself, that which enables beings to be. On this point Macquarrie stands near Tillich, who wrote: "However it is defined, the 'existence of God' contradicts the idea of a creative ground of essence and existence. The ground of being cannot be found within the totality of beings, nor can the ground of essence and existence participate in the tensions and disruptions characteristic of the transition from essence to existence."[16]

In further developing the idea of existence with reference to God, however, Macquarrie adds qualifications that may at times obscure his intent. He writes:

> But to let be is more primordial than to be, so that, as already has been said, being 'is' more 'beingful' than any possible being which it lets be; and this justifies us using such expressions as 'being is,' provided we remain aware of their logically 'stretched' character. . . . So it can be asserted that, while to say 'God exists' is strictly inaccurate and may be misleading if it makes us think of him as *some* being or other, yet it is more appropriate to say 'God exists' than 'God does not exist,' since God's letting-be is prior to and the condition of the existence of any particular being.[17]

In the second edition of *Principles,* a paragraph is added that is intended to elaborate on these qualifications and respond to critics. In it Macquarrie says that "being," "is," and "exists" can be used analogically with reference to God, and to illustrate this he gives an example of what we have called exists$_2$:

> If I say that man 'exists' in the sense that Sartre and others say this, the word has a very active sense and indicates man separating himself from nature and choosing his own essence. But if I say God 'exists,' then the dynamic, active sense of existing is raised to a new unimaginable level and the limitations of human existence are discarded. Provided that one is clear that the word 'exists' (or 'is') has an entire range of meanings, then it is appropriate to say 'God exists'.[18]

The addition of these qualifications creates some problems, but in general it might be said that while Macquarrie is sympathetic with Tillich's argument, he stands closer to the position of H. J. Paton, who in his Gifford lectures said he saw no need to be dogmatic on this issue, that if the word "exists" is understood to apply only to finite things in time and space, then it is inappropriate to say "God exists," but that one may say "God exists" if one makes it clear that "exists" is being used in some analogical sense.[19]

A further complication is introduced later on in *Principles*, however, when Macquarrie writes:

> The assertion 'God exists' is not to be taken as meaning that there is to be found a being possessing such and such characteristics. 'God exists' is a way of asserting what would perhaps be more exactly expressed as the holiness of being. But it is precisely the assertion of the holiness of being which is denied by atheism, so that our manner of interpreting the expression 'God exists' in terms of God as being makes not the slightest concession to atheism. It does, however, rule out obsolete and untenable mythological and metaphysical ways of thinking of God.[20]

Macquarrie is suggesting that the debate between theists and atheists should no longer center on the question "Does God exist?" but on the question "Is Being gracious?"[21] This is an important and fundamental shift in the way of looking at the question of God. It suggests a more subtle understanding of the difference between atheism and theism than is contained in the traditional formula that theists affirm and atheists deny that God exists. Unfortunately, Macquarrie's tendency at times to blur the distinction between exists$_1$ and exists$_2$ may obscure this shift. To say that "God exists" means "Being is holy" is to do more than stretch the meaning of "exists." It is to judge inappropriate the traditional way of thinking and speaking of God. We must therefore clarify Macquarrie's perspective on the question of God while we examine further what he means to say regarding God's existence.[22]

First, within the context of Macquarrie's thought one can continue to speak of the existence (exists$_2$) of God on the grounds that while God is not a being, God enables beings to be and is manifest in them. In this case, however, we must keep clearly in mind that "exists" is being used in a descriptive and analogical sense and that, to be informative, our verbs should be interpreted by terms that indicate specific ways God functions or behaves. One may, for example, by analogy to human existence, speak of God's love or historicity. Second, one may give up talk about the existence of God in the sense of exists$_1$. Granted that exists$_1$ is used in a variety of contexts (for example, with reference to tables, electrons, ideas, and persons) and that the criteria for accepting something as existing will differ, such sentences as "There exists an instance of X" refer to entities existing in space and time, and it is difficult to conceive of sentences using exists$_1$ that can avoid this connotation. Yet Being or God is said not to be an entity and thus not a part of the totality of that which exists (exists$_1$).

How does this analysis of the term "existence" fit Macquarrie's way of talking about God? If God is understood in the mythological sense, it may be appropriate to ask, "Does God exist?" Macquarrie, however, argues that we have passed beyond the mythological stage of traditional theism in so far as it conceived of God as a person, albeit an odd, metaphysical kind of person who dwelt metaphorically beyond the world, intervening as necessary.[23] It is granted that traditional theists do not speak of the existence of God in any straightforward sense. In traditional theism, God is spoken of as a being, but the difference between God and other entities is stressed, and frequent reference is made to God's necessary existence, suggesting that "existence," when applied to God, is a qualified term. But talk of God's existing or not is made more ambiguous whenever it is stressed that God is immeasurably the greatest being and different from all particular beings.

Although Macquarrie argues that we have passed beyond traditional theism, he admits, as we have said, that he stands close to the tradition of the Greek Fathers, St. Augustine, and St. Thomas in associating the idea of God with the idea of Being. He argues, however, that we must now assert unambiguously that God is not a being, not even immeasurably the greatest being, but Being itself. If Macquarrie wishes to make that assertion, however, he should also assert unambiguously that one should not use "exists$_1$" in reference to God, because such usage blurs the very distinction he wishes to maintain. Presumably, each thing that exists, exists as something, but God understood as Being cannot be said to exist as something.

If one does reject exists₁ as inappropriate in reference to God, it becomes easier to understand Macquarrie's claim that the real issue between theists and atheists is not the existence or non-existence of God but whether the character of Being is gracious or alien. Macquarrie does not intend his reformulation of the issue to rule out questions of truth or falsity with respect to religious claims. In addressing such questions, he places primary emphasis on describing the experience of Being, but also argues that a theistic theory gives a better account of the data of experience than do atheistic theories. Macquarrie does not suggest that all persons who understand Being as gracious are theists. He does suggest that the line between theists and atheists cannot be drawn as sharply as it could when the question was one of merely affirming or denying the existence of some divine entity in addition to all the other entities that make up what we call world.

This shift from talk about the existence of God to talk about the nature of Being is consistent with Macquarrie's shift from understanding God as a transcendent entity to understanding God as Being. The correspondence is suggested in Macquarrie's discussion of Wisdom's parable concerning the garden and the gardener. Wisdom's parable begins, says Macquarrie, as a useful illustration of the traditional way of discussing whether God exists, the traditional discussion between theists and atheists. But, says Macquarrie, a shift in the parable occurs that has not been readily noted and that is parallel to the shift from the classical type of theism to one which takes more seriously the immanence of God in the world and his relation to it.

> They begin by returning to their neglected garden, and the question at issue is whether a gardener comes to tend it. This seems to represent the dispute between classical theism and the corresponding atheism. But not much further on, the grounds of the dispute have shifted and the argument takes a different form. Now one man says to the other, 'You still think the world's a garden and not a wilderness.' Here the argument is no longer about the question of the gardener who may or may not come to tend the plot. It has become an argument about the character of the plot of ground itself—whether or not it is a garden. As the argument proceeds, it seems to assume increasingly the second form. It becomes less and less an

argument as to whether *there* is a gardener, separate from the garden and coming and going at will, and it becomes more and more a question as to whether the plot displays such a character as would constitute it a garden, or whether it must be reckoned a wilderness. The checking procedures differ also. For there is less and less talk about the possibility of hearing, seeing or detecting a gardener at work, and more and more talk about the immanent characteristics of the plot of ground, and especially whether one can trace in it what might be called the pattern of gardenhood.[24]

Macquarrie's primary purpose in this passage is to illustrate the difference between the classical or monarchical type of theism (where God's transcendence and priority over the world have been central) and an organic view of God (where the relation between God and world is understood to be much more intimate). Macquarrie adopts what he calls an "organic model" for God as a corrective to the monarchical model. While his view differs from those of Alexander, Whitehead, and Hartshorne, Macquarrie makes it clear that he shares much in common with them. His interpretation of the parable, with the focus moving from concern over the gardener's arriving (God's existence) to concern with the character of the garden itself, dramatizes Macquarrie's shift in the way of talking about God. As one becomes aware of the limits of the traditional question of the existence of God, one senses that the need to confront the issue of God's reality in another way is crucial. The question now has to do with the most appropriate way of describing our experience of reality. It is not that the theist sees something the atheist does not see. It is rather that the two pattern their experiences in different ways and argue whether talk of God or of the holiness of Being can be justified in the effort to account for experience.

At this point the debate between theists and atheists may appear to be reduced to a debate between the followers of Jaspers or Heidegger and the followers of Sartre or Camus. Many atheists, one might argue, are not concerned with the nature of Being. They say simply that things are and that there is no justification for arguing about the character of Being.[25]

The point is well taken and characterizes the empirical sensibility and its absence of interest in metaphysical questions. If one consistently maintains this position, there is probably little room for serious dialogue between theists and atheists. But neither Macquarrie nor Heidegger is unaware of this. Indeed, it is the intent of Macquarrie's natural theology that one begin at this point in order to show the importance of the question of Being. The question of Being, as Macquarrie understands it, is not so much concerned with giving a rationalistic account of Being as it with asking about the meaning of Being for human existence.

It should be clear now why Macquarrie, having set aside talk of God as a being who created the world, exercises control over it, and intervenes on occasions, is reluctant to talk about the existence of God. God is not an entity existing independently of the world. God enables beings to be and is manifest in them. For this reason, some interpreters regard Macquarrie as a pantheist, in spite of his emphasis on the transcendence of God. But even though Macquarrie argues for an organic view of the relation between God and the world, his view is not pantheistic. The term "panentheistic" is more appropriate, and Macquarrie himself uses it in describing his position. Panentheism is an alternative both to theistic dualism and to pantheistic monism and is defined in *The Oxford Dictionary of the Christian Church* as "the belief that the Being of God includes and penetrates the whole universe, so that every part of it exists in him, but (as against pantheism) that this Being is more than, and is not exhausted by, the universe."

God, understood as Holy Being, is said by Macquarrie to be other than and ontologically prior to the world. God enables or lets-be persons and things in the world. Macquarrie's organic model does not abolish the traditional theistic idea of the transcendence and priority of God, but qualifies it by seeing God and world as distinguishable but not separable within an organic whole. Macquarrie's model permits an interdependence of God and world, so that God who is outgoing love cannot be conceived of without a creation and so that God is in some sense vulnerable to or affected by creation as well as affecting it.[26]

We have seen that Macquarrie's primary model for explaining the relation of God and world is the relation between Being and beings. He also uses the relation of form to matter as a model. But "form" is not conceived of in the Platonic sense as eternal and unchanging. "Form," in Macquarrie's view, is more closely associated with Heidegger's understanding of the temporality of human existence. "In this case the form is, as it were, an active *Gestalt,* informing the body and expressing itself in and through the body."[27] Macquarrie cautions us against interpreting the terms "form" and "body" in a literal sense. He recognizes that the physical world differs from the body of a living creature and notes that God not only informs the world but brings it into being. God is creative form. Also, "form" should not suggest an ordered universe only but should take into account the personal and historical. Given those caveats, however, Macquarrie *believes the Aristotelian model of form and matter* useful in suggesting the intimacy of the relation between God and world. God is thought of as "creative living form, a dynamic reality giving being, direction, and intelligibility to the world."[28] Here the transcendence of God meets the freedom and creativity of man. God becomes, in the words of Charles Hartshorne that Macquarrie quotes with sympathy, "the unsurpassing inspiring genius of all freedom, not the all-determining coercive tyrant."[29]

The direction in which he is moving is fairly clear. Traditional conceptions of God as substance have followed consciously or unconsciously the dualistic Platonic model of selfhood. However, now that we find it difficult to hold concepts of a disembodied self or soul, we also find it difficult to conceive of God as a transcendent being, a substance separate from the world but which provides it with unity and stability. The self, and by analogy God, cannot be conceived of adequately using the model of subpersonal being. The self, as Macquarrie understands it, is a dynamic, creative, embodied form inseparable from the body. The term "self" may be said to refer to the bringing to fulfillment of those potentialities provided in its embodied existence in the world. The self is manifested in its activity, in its way of being in the world.[30]

For Heidegger, as we recall, the Being of human existence is ultimately expressed in terms of temporality, and Heidegger himself suggests that the eternity of God might be conceived of as a more primordial infinite temporality.[31] According to Heidegger, things *are* to the extent that they endure through past, present, and future. Human existence may understand itself in time in this way as merely a thing whose unity is one in which past, present, and future are only causally related to it. The authentic understanding of human existence, however, is one in which past, present, and future are seen in terms of my possibilities of being. It is characteristic of my existence that I stand before my future possibilities, that I am also my past, and that I stand in the tension between past and future in the present. Persons differ from other entities in that they are aware of the present but also remember the past and anticipate the future. In authentic existence, present, past, and future are brought into a unity. In inauthentic existence, there is no unity, and the self merely endures through past, present, and future.

When the substance model for talking about God is replaced by the existentialist model of human existence, temporality becomes fundamental in talking about God. As we are not merely in time but take past, present, and future into our way of being, so by analogy God who is understood as Being or Holy Being is not merely in time but takes time into himself. As Macquarrie puts it:

> If Being is, as Heidegger expresses it, "the *transcendens* pure and simple," then it is more appropriate to say that history (and also time) are "in" Being rather than that Being is in time and history. Yet insofar as Being includes becoming, it has taken time into itself, and manifests itself in time and history; more than this, it expands and realizes itself in history, more and more unfolding its resources. Just as the trinitarian symbols, while indeed reflecting the community's temporal or historical experience of God, nevertheless point to something in God himself, so time and history are not just forms under which we perceive a timeless and non-historical Being. They really belong to Being, and without them Being could not be dynamic, it could not manifest itself, it could not be God or Holy Being; it could be only an inert static Being, and about this we would know nothing for we ourselves would not *be*. But Being is not *in* time and history, as if these were more ultimate than Being. Rather, the expansion and expression of Being creates time and history.[32]

Macquarrie's argument is that as selfhood is the bringing

into unity of the dimensions of past, present, and future through remembering the past, projecting into the future, and being open to both in the present, so God or Holy Being can be understood as realizing himself in the ecstasies of past, present, and future. As the self is not merely a series of nows but a unity of past, present, and future, so God is a unity of past, present, and future. Without this process of realization and manifestation, Being or God would remain, as Hegel suggested, simple and indeterminate. So we can visualize, says Macquarrie,

> the emergence of primordial Being through expressive Being into time and history, yet in such a way that through its self-outpouring from its original unbroken unity, a new and richer unity is being all the time built up through unitive Being, a unity that with every creative outpouring becomes richer and fuller still. The end would be all things gathered up into God, all things brought to the fulfillment of their potentialities for being, at one among themselves and at one with Being from which they have come and for which they are destined. But this end too could not be thought of as a point that will eventually be reached, for at every point new vistas will open up. Being must remain at once stable and dynamic.[33]

Macquarrie recognizes the parallels between his understanding of God and Hegel's understanding of Absolute Spirit, but he does not believe that his theory results, as it did for Hegel, in a loss of individual selfhood. There is a sense, he argues, in which the absorption of the individual into the whole might seem to follow from the idea of the fulfillment of individual being understood as the outpouring love of God. But a theory that resulted in the absorption of the individual would, he argues, make pointless the notion of creation. The process of things being gathered up into God makes sense only if that which is advancing in its creative potentialities leads to a more fully diversified unity. "The end, we have seen reason to believe, would be a commonwealth of free responsible beings united in love; and this great end is possible only if finite existents are preserved in some kind of individual identity."[34]

We see now how Macquarrie's organic theory of God or Holy Being differs from the substance theory of classical theism. What Macquarrie proposes is a theory of God that stresses the infinite temporality of God and the intimate relation between God and world without forgoing the emphasis on God's transcendence. God is understood by Macquarrie as Being, the *transcendens,* who is nevertheless in the world in relation to persons and things. God is understood as the Being of beings, or the form of the world, who in his structure is related to his creation. As my being in the world in relation to persons and things is not accidental to my being, so God's being in the world in relation to persons and things is not accidental to God. The relation of God to his creation is part of the essential structure of God. This idea distinguishes Macquarrie's idea of God from the concept of God in classical theism.

Macquarrie also departs from classical theism by rejecting the notion of God as timeless. Temporality is characteristic of God in the sense that the ecstasies of time are said to be taken up into God and that in the end all things are said to have their potentialities in him. This is not to say that God is temporal in the same sense that man is temporal. Unlike man, God has neither beginning nor end. God is not a being with a particular past and particular future. Rather, the past and the future of God are without limit, and in God all things have their beginning and are brought to the fulfillment of their potentialities.

Macquarrie's theory of God helps overcome some of the difficulties in classical theistic theories and promises to give a more adequate account of the Biblical understanding of God than most alternatives provide. But in what sense can we have knowledge of God? That is the topic of the next chapter.

Notes

1. *Thinking About God,* pp. 90–91.
2. *Thinking About God,* p. 91; and Schubert Ogden, *The Reality of God* (New York: Harper and Row, 1966), p. 37.
3. *Thinking About God,* p. 106.
4. *Principles,* p. 107.
5. *Principles,* pp. 107ff. See Martin Heidegger, *Being and Time,* pp. 2ff., 38ff.
6. *Principles,* p. 109.
7. *Thinking About God,* p. 96.
8. *Thinking About God,* p. 107; and *Principles,* pp. 196–97.
9. *Principles,* p. 113.
10. Yeow Choo Lak, *Singaporean Glimpses of Macquarrie on Revelation* (Singapore: Trinity Theological College, 1977), p. 29.
11. *Principles,* pp. 114–115. *The Humility of God* (London: SCM Press, 1978), pp. 1ff.
12. *Principles,* p. 115.
13. H. P. Owen, *Concepts of Deity* (London: Macmillan, 1971), p. 140.
14. Milton K. Munitz, *The Mystery of Existence* (New York: Appleton Century-Crofts, 1965), pp. 72–99.
15. *Principles,* p. 118.
16. Paul Tillich, *Systematic Theology,* Vol. I (Chicago: The University of Chicago Press, 1951), pp. 204–205.
17. *Principles,* p. 118.
18. *Principles,* p. 119.
19. H. J. Paton, *The Modern Predicament* (London: Allen and Unwin, 1955).
20. *Principles,* p. 120.
21. *Thinking About God,* pp. 90–95.
22. John Robinson analyses the question of God in a similar way, arguing that we have already recognized this in talk of the devil: *Exploration Into God* (London and Oxford: Mowbrays, 1977), p. 36. For some interesting parallels, see Stewart Sutherland's study of Dostoyevsky: *Atheism and the Rejection of God* (Oxford: Basil Blackwell, 1977).
23. *Thinking About God,* pp. 99ff.
24. *Thinking About God,* p. 115.
25. Alister Kee, *The Way of Transcendence* (Middlesex: Penguin Books, 1971), pp. 45ff.
26. *Thinking About God,* p. 114.

27. *Thinking About God,* p. 117.
28. *Thinking About God,* p. 118.
29. *In Search of Humanity,* Chapter III.
30. *Studies,* pp. 62ff.
31. *Being and Time,* p. 499, n. xiii. I discuss this in some detail in "God and Temporality: A Heideggerian View." *God and Temporality,* ed. Bowman Clarke and Eugene Long (New York: Paragon House Publishers, 1984), pp. 121–32.
32. *Principles,* p. 208.
33. *Principles,* p. 359.
34. *Principles,* p. 360.

4

KNOWLEDGE
OF GOD

THERE HAVE BEEN TWO FUNDAMENTAL APPROACHES TO KNOWL-edge of God in the history of Western thought. The rationalist approach, which places primary emphasis on reason and argument, generally thinks of God as an inferred entity and of religious faith as the acceptance of a theistic hypothesis. The experiential approach claims that rational arguments have no compelling force when taken independently of religious experience and insists that religious faith is a commitment that differs in kind from the tentative commitment associated with the acceptance of a hypothesis.

Since the nineteenth century the experiential approach has been central to discussions of religious knowledge and has brought, some would argue, a more significant understanding of religion. At times, however, this emphasis on experience has led to a repudiation of any role for argument, with the result that questions of justification have been inadequately treated. Friedrich Schleiermacher, for one, runs this risk when he argues that the feeling of absolute dependence "entirely takes the place . . . of all the so-called proofs of the existence of God."[1] And many twentieth-century thinkers influenced by the existentialists have tended to emphasize faith in God at the expense of knowledge about God. Thus, Martin Buber has claimed, "It is not necessary to know something about God in order to really believe in Him."[2]

Macquarrie has much in common with such nineteenth-century thinkers as Schleiermacher, and he has been influenced by the existentialists and their emphasis on knowledge by participation. However, while he emphasizes the role of experience and faith in religious knowledge, he insists that faith *in* God requires knowledge *about* God and that reason and argument have a role to play in religious knowledge. One might classify Macquarrie's approach to knowledge as empirical, in the broader sense of that term, although he is somewhat reluctant to classify himself as an empiricist. It is clear that he differs from so-called classical empiricists, who equate experience with sense experience downplaying inner experiences, and who limit knowledge to objective and universally valid claims. Regarding experience Macquarrie is closer to the pragmatists and phenomenologists. He prefers to speak of a human concept of knowledge, based on more than sense experience, a concept consistent with a wide range of human experience of reality, including the moral, the interpersonal, the aesthetic, and the religious.

Macquarrie does not provide us with a theory of experience, and at times this creates some difficulties in understanding what he means by the term. He seems more intent on pointing to several kinds of experience. For example, instead of arguing for a theory of experience as "encountering" rather than "undergoing," as some have done in an effort to avoid the claim that appeals to experience are merely subjective, he seems to accept that there are different kinds of experience, some for which the term "observing" is appropriate and others for which the terms "encountering" and "undergoing" are appropriate. Yet it is clear that he is in essential agreement with those who argue that experience is not merely subjective, that it is intentional in character, and that it takes place in a context in which persons are already related to persons and things in the world.

Since the time of Kant, Macquarrie argues, it has been clear that we hardly ever confront so-called raw experience. Experience is always interpreted. Macquarrie is here echoing Heidegger, who wrote, "What we 'first' hear is never noises or complexes of sounds, but the creaking wagon, the motorcycle. We hear the column on the march, the north wind, the woodpecker tapping, the fire crackling. It requires a very artificial and complicated frame of mind to 'hear' a 'pure noise'."[3] Heidegger takes this as evidence that human existence is in every case already in the world alongside what is understood, that one does not have to leap from experience to the world, as some of the more subjective views of experience seem to suggest. This means that experiencing involves some kind of reciprocal relationship between us and the world and that interpreting, and we might add understanding and explaining, are not activities contrary to experience. Interpreting is in fact basic to our efforts to articulate our encounters with persons and things in the world.

It is not always easy to fit Macquarrie's references to "inner experience" and his emphasis on the passivity of some types of experience into this scheme. But his talk of experience does seem consistent with the theory outlined here. He understands experience to be intentional in structure, to involve interpretation, and to take place in the context of our being already in the world, in relation to persons and things. And he argues that experience can never be self-authenticating. If there is always interpretation, there is always the risk of misinterpretation, so that we must provide for discussions and arguments about the adequacy of our interpretations.

Some contemporary thinkers who share Macquarrie's view of the relation between experience and interpretation have argued that there are no distinctive religious experiences, that the same data are present for both the religious and the non-religious interpreter, and that only differing schemes for interpreting the data are at issue. This view, however, often leads to conceptual relativism. Religious faith becomes little more than having a particular perspective or seeing the data in a particular way.

To avoid conceptual relativism, some religious thinkers have insisted on a distinctive religious experience. H. D. Lewis, for example, argues that theists have an intuition of the transcendent that is different from experiences that are neutral regarding religious or non-religious interpretations. For Lewis this intuition, or "enlivened sense of the being of God," is compelling for the person having it. It is the intuition of a positive, transcendent, and irreducible mystery that is filled out in association with historical religious experience.[4]

Although Macquarrie would not insist on anything like Lewis's compelling intuition, he believes that the religious or transcendent dimensions in ordinary experience would not be recognized without distinctive religious experiences. He also believes that just as one cannot understand much about art without some artistic sensibility, one cannot understand much about religion without some sensibility toward the holy. Macquarrie agrees with those who want to insist on the importance of distinctively religious experience but he does not believe that such experience is compelling or self-authenticating.

What, then, is this distinctively religious experience to which Macquarrie refers? In one place he suggests that it is "very diverse and includes worship, conversion, mysticism, spirit possession and so on. The appeal to distinctively religious experience is basic to the thought of Schleiermacher and Otto and is believed by them to give assurance of the presence and reality of God or of the holy."[5] Elsewhere, he speaks of this experience in terms of Otto's analysis of the numinous and of Schleiermacher's "feeling of absolute dependence," and seems to emphasize man's being mastered by and passive before the numinous reality. In *Principles of Christian Theology,* he associates Otto's analysis of the numinous with "holy Being." By distinctively religious experience Macquarrie means an experience of ultimacy or holiness in the presence of Being understood as gracious. Religious experiences in the distinctive sense, however, are not different in kind from the experience of ultimacy or holiness in ordinary experiences. With Peter Berger and Langdon Gilkey, Macquarrie agrees that there is a depth or sense of ultimacy in ordinary experience. He insists, however, that "there are indeed distinctively religious experiences in which there is concentrated what is present in a more peripheral way in ordinary experience," and that without the specifically religious experiences as described by Otto we would not place a religious interpretation on the "religious dimensions" of ordinary experience.[6]

Distinctively religious experiences, then, disclose the presence of Holy Being or God. The term "revelation" is considered by many theologians to refer to the distinctively religious experience. As understood by Macquarrie, revelation is not so much a category of experience as a particular mode of religious experience. That is, one can say of our everyday experiences of transcendence or the holy that they have a revelatory element, but it is unlikely that we could understand what the theologian means by "revelation" unless we had some experience of transcendence which bears an analogy to revelation.

Although the term "revelation" may refer to experiences other than distinctively religious ones, it is most typically associated with religious experience in the strict sense, and communities of faith trace their origins to what Macquarrie calls a classic or primordial revelation, a "definite disclosive experience of the holy granted to the founder or founders of the community."[7] In being repeated or re-enacted in the community primordial revelation becomes normative for the experience of the community. The present experience of the community is submitted to the relatively objective content of the primordial revelation on which the community is founded. This need not mean, however, that revelation is authoritatively laid before us in the Scripture and tradition of a community of faith. The Scripture and tradition of a community may be said to re-present the primordial revelation in the context of the present experience of the community of faith. Thus, each generation must appropriate its Scripture and tradition, reinterpreting them in view of its present experience.

By "revelation," Macquarrie means in the strict sense the experience of Holy Being within the context of a community of faith. It points, he says, especially to the cognitive element in the experience of man's understanding of himself and the wider being in which he has his being. But what is the cognitive nature of this revelatory experience and how does it relate to other cognitive experiences? In its most general sense "revelation" refers to the disclosure of what is otherwise known or hidden to us. It may refer to the disclosure of some new information, as when we say after a lecture, "That was a revelation to me." It may also refer to my coming to understand myself or another person in a new way. In this case information is involved, but the emphasis is on some change that takes place in the way that I understand myself or others.

The distinction that is made in ordinary discourse between revelation as disclosing new information and revelation as bringing about a new understanding of myself and others is also apparent in the religious context. Indeed, the difference between the propositional and non-propositional views of revelation is based on this difference. In the former case it is argued that revelation refers to the disclosure of a set of propositions and in the latter case it is argued that God himself is disclosed. However, the difference between the two views is at times exaggerated. St. Thomas, for example, with whom the classical, propositional view of revelation is frequently associated, believes that the ultimate object of faith is God himself, and theologians such as Rudolf Bultmann, with whom the non-propositional view is associated, will agree that information is always involved in coming to a new understanding of oneself in relation to God. Macquarrie, like Bultmann, emphasizes the revelation of God as a new self-understanding, but argues that this is intelligible only if the person to whom God is revealed is also aware of some truths about God.

The fundamental difference between these two views is not that in one case faith involves belief in a set of propositions and in the other case it does not. The difference is that in one case it is believed that the propositions of revelation are ready-made statements to which the religious person is to give assent, and in the other case the propositions represent attempts to give expression to the disclosure of God which ultimately lies beyond our verbal formulations of it.

Although much of the emphasis in discussions of revelation is placed on the initiative of God, revelation is not, according to Macquarrie, an arbitrary event. There are two sides to the revelatory situation. The revelation of God is in some sense a response to the human quest for meaning in existence. In our earlier discussion of Macquarrie's understanding of existence and Being, we were describing the human side of the revelatory situation. Faced with the polarities in our experience of existence and Being, and in particular with the experience of anxiety, two possibilities are confronted, the absurdity of existence or our being given to ourselves from beyond ourselves. The mood of anxiety, says Macquarrie, constitutes

> our capacity for receiving revelation. It predisposes us to recognize the approach of holy being. In other words, I am asserting a continuity between the quest for sense and

grace that rises out of man's existence, and the direc-
tionally opposite *quest for man*, to which experiences of
grace and revelation bear witness, a quest that is initiated
outside of man and remains beyond his control.[8]

It is, then, against the awareness of our being and toward
the nullity of our existence that man is said to become aware of
the revelation or disclosure of Being. Heidegger argues that
since thinking begins with beings or entities within the world,
Being that is not an entity must first be encountered as a
negative, a no-thing. But for those who do not arbitrarily limit
their inquiry at this point, nothing is seen to pertain to Being in
that it discloses beings as beings. "Being" in this sense is the
condition that there be beings at all. Macquarrie finds a parallel
description of the disclosure of Being in Rudolf Otto's *The Idea
of the Holy*. Otto's "creaturely feeling" is said to parallel the notion
of anxiety, which becomes awe in the face of the holy. In Otto's
analysis of this experience in terms of the *mysterium tremendum et
fascinans*, the *mysterium* refers to the incomprehensible depth of the
numinous presence of that which is other than beings in the
world. The term *tremendum* stresses the otherness of Being over
against the finiteness of our existence, and *fascinans* refers to what
we called earlier the grace of Being, the source of the fulfillment
of our existence.

According to Macquarrie, revelation in the religious sense is
the disclosure of Being or God. It is against the nullity of all
beings that Being is encountered and understood. Revelation
involves a transformation of vision, a new understanding of
ourselves in relation to Being. At times Macquarrie speaks of this
revelation as seeing the same things in a different way. He does
not mean by this, however, that revelation is merely a "blik," a
way of looking at the world. He means that in the revelatory
situation a person's attention is drawn to some features that
might otherwise be overlooked.

Revelation in this sense may be said to be direct. It is not the
result of some inference. But it is not immediate. If it were, it
would be independent of the interpretation of experience by
which the person having the revelation discovers the import of
the event on his life. Revelation in Macquarrie's sense is a dimension within the experience of man as a being in the world. As such

it is not a merely subjective experience but involves a reciprocal relationship between what is given and a person and requires an interpretive act on his part. Understanding and interpreting are not activities independent of the disclosure of Being but are integral parts of our efforts to articulate the disclosure of Being in our encounters with persons and things in the world.

Macquarrie suggests that there are parallels between the kind of understanding or knowing that occurs in religious revelatory experience and the kind of understanding that takes place in aesthetic and moral experience. Aesthetic thinking, according to him, is not merely a matter of technical reasoning, although that is certainly involved. It involves the response of our whole existence. What is known is not something in addition to or behind our ordinary ways of knowing the art object, but a depth of what confronts us, a structure or gestalt that is noticed in experiencing the art object. Aesthetic awareness, he argues, has a gift like character, "for the 'beautiful' or the 'sublime,' like the 'holy' or the 'numinous,' seems to take possession of us."[9] The artist often describes inspiration in these terms. Similarly, one may recognize in moral experience a claim set over against oneself which has a character of otherness and ultimacy that cannot be fully accounted for by reference to the demands of society upon us. Indeed, the moral claim seems at times to stand in judgment on ourselves and society.

Macquarrie intends that the revelatory experience be understood as cognitive, but in what sense is it appropriate to speak of revelation as a form of cognition? Here Macquarrie appeals to Heidegger's distinction between calculative and meditative thinking.[10] According to Heidegger, calculative thinking is the kind of thinking prevalent in scientific and scholarly investigations. It is the activity of understanding in which we separate object from subject. Essential to this type of thinking is an act of will that permits the thinker to transcend and in some sense control the object of his thinking. The thinker makes experience conform to his productive relations within the world. Calculative thinking reaches its extreme in the world of technology, where we use or manipulate things in order to attain some desired result. Heidegger understands technology and calculative thinking to be rooted in traditional metaphysics, which reached its culmination in Nietzsche's metaphysics of the will.

By contrast, meditative thinking is a stepping-back from things in order that they may disclose themselves in their Being. Thinking in this sense is the opposite of calculative thinking, which seeks to make the world conform to its grasping concepts. Meditative thinking entails an openness toward things that lets them be as they are. Meditative thinking is not, as some critics have suggested, merely passive. It includes a questioning penetration of the given, a moving beyond our preoccupation with beings as objects. But meditative thinking is said to be ultimately realized only in the disclosure of Being, an event which cannot be controlled or determined by us but for which we must in some sense wait.

Calculative thinking, as Macquarrie suggests, is the kind of thinking we associate with the expression "objective knowledge." Neither Macquarrie nor Heidegger wishes to reject the importance of this way of thinking about the world. Macquarrie, however, is critical of those who make calculative thinking the paradigm of all thinking and who ignore many dimensions of our response to existence and Being or reduce them to the realm of the non-cognitive. It was against the dominance of the calculative thinking model that the existentialists revolted, calling for a mode of thinking appropriate to personal existence. The thinker reflecting on human existence was understood by the existentialists to be not a spectator but an actor, a participant who shared with others a personal being that broke through the limits of mere objective knowledge. This approach to knowledge reached its limits perhaps in Martin Buber's I-thou relation, where emphasis was placed on the kind of knowing of others in which we are dependent on the other's letting himself be known. This personal model of knowing was extended by some to thinking about Being or God. Macquarrie, as we shall see, criticizes the personal model for knowledge of God, but he believes it does move us further toward an appreciation and understanding of the personal dimension of the experience of existence and Being.

One can understand why this personal model of thinking and knowing was so influential on theologians. In the revelatory situation, the religious believer is dependent upon the disclosure of God in much the same way that persons are dependent on the self-disclosure of other persons. Macquarrie expresses appreciation for the analogy between knowledge of God and knowledge of persons but argues that there are three limitations to the analogy that makes it inadequate: (1) the encounter of persons with God and the encounter of persons with other persons are different, the latter being contingent on some actual physical entity; (2) the essential character of the reciprocity that is central to I-person encounters does not seem equally appropriate to the revelatory situation, in which persons are utterly transcended by Being that reveals itself; and (3) personal knowledge speaks of a knowing by one person of another, whereas with revelation we are said to know not another being but Being itself, that which is no-thing in relation to all other entities.[11]

Although Macquarrie's criticisms of this personal mode of thinking and knowing may seem to suggest that he rejects the mediation of Being in the world in favor of some kind of immediate and passive encounter with Being, this is not his intention. Further analysis of Heidegger's model of meditative thinking, which Macquarrie adopts in his understanding of the cognitive dimension of revelatory thinking, should make his intention clear.

Meditative thinking, in Heidegger's sense, has the task of thinking about that which is implicit in, but hidden to, the world of calculative thinking. In *Discourse on Thinking,* Heidegger expresses this comportment toward calculative thinking as saying simultaneously a "Yes" and a "No." Meditative thinking is a way of life whereby we live within the world of calculative thinking, advance it, profit from it, and yet are not bound by it. Meditative thinking neither denies the validity of calculative thinking nor seeks to escape from it. Rather, it seeks to move beyond the limiting prejudgments implicit in calculative thinking in order to think about that which is presupposed in it and therefore not available to it. To put it another way, whereas in calculative thinking we veil the ontological difference between Being and beings and come to rest upon beings, in meditative thinking we are directed to think the ontological difference.

Meditative thinking entails a new comportment toward things. In the final analysis, as we shall see, this new comportment or vision is not something accomplished merely by our decision. The thinker however, is not totally inactive. Meditative thinking requires an act of non-willing, a willing renunciation of willing in which we stand open to the possibility of release into the emergence of the hidden meaning of things. As scientist says to teacher in Heidegger's essay, "Conversation on a Country Path about Thinking": "You must want a non-willing in the sense of a renouncing of willing, so that through this we may release, or at least prepare to release, ourselves to that sought-for essence of a thinking that is not a willing."[12] In practice, this act of non-willing is a questioning, inquiring attitude in which beings in their Being can remain problematical, something to be sought; it is the attitude suggested by Aristotle but often falsified by his followers.

If, however, meditative thinking entails this act of non-willing, this act cannot of its own volition awaken or accomplish releasement and openness to Being. Thinking, as Heidegger says in *Das Ding,* is not a mere change of attitude. The willing not to will is essential in keeping us awake to releasement and thinking, but this thinking ultimately comes as a gift. For this reason Heidegger maintains that releasement is beyond both passivity and activity on the part of the thinker.

Heidegger makes this same point in a different way in *An Introduction to Metaphysics.* Here we learn that the purpose of Heidegger's asking of another, "Why are there beings rather than nothing?" is to awaken a questioning state of mind, a willing to know rather than a striving to know. Heidegger intends by this to put the emphasis on the more passive aspect of knowing. To will to know is in this sense to be resolved, to let oneself be summoned out of fallenness or irresoluteness, in which knowing is equated with having information and truth with the correspondence of a judgment with its object. The etymological connection in the German language between resoluteness (*Entschlossenheit*) and disclosedness (*Erschlossenheit*) underlines the correlation. To will to know is to be resolved, where resoluteness has to do with the opening of human existence into the clearing of the disclosure of Being. Willing to know is thus grounded in letting-be, a standing in the disclosure of Being.[13]

Implicit in this understanding of meditative thinking is a dialectic between questioning and paying heed to or shepherding the disclosure of Being. This dialectic resembles the one Karl Jaspers suggests between *Verstand* (Intellect) and *Vernunft* (Reason). Calculative thinking, according to Heidegger, is not something that can be extended into meditative thinking. Meditative thinking is said to occur in a leap of vision, or openness to the presence of Being. Yet this change of vision never takes place independently of a slow and consistent process of interrogation of what is given.

If there is a formal mode for this thinking, it is the questioning that never comes to rest in statements of information, that strips off the layers of things and words, and that prepares us for the change of vision in which we are open and give heed to the disclosure of Being. Heidegger suggests an analogy between this mode of thinking and the apprenticeship of a cabinetmaker. Certainly the cabinetmaker is not merely passive. He brings with him his skill in the use of tools. Yet, says Heidegger, if the apprentice cabinetmaker is to learn his craft, he must do more than practice the manipulation of tools in order to produce things conforming to customary patterns. If he is to be a true cabinetmaker, he must learn to respond to the different kinds of wood, to the shapes that lie hidden in the wood. Otherwise, his cabinetmaking, and by analogy his thinking, would be no more than a technical undertaking and his work might be little more than meaningless busywork.[14]

To Heidegger then, meditative thinking begins with an understanding of beings in the world, but the thinker stands open to the disclosure of beings as beings, to the address of Being, in which the ontological difference between beings and Being is disclosed. This mode of thinking, suggests Macquarrie, provides a paradigm for understanding what is meant by revelation, showing where revelation is located in the range of man's cognitive experience. In both cases the initiative shifts to what is disclosed, to what is known. Yet what is known in this case is not another being but Being itself, Being as disclosed through the particular beings by which Being itself is present. The knowledge of Being or God has a gift-like character, which the religious person refers to in speaking of revealed knowledge and of man's dependence on the initiative of the divine. For Macquarrie, as for Heidegger, however, we are not merely passive recipients of this disclosure. Knowing, writes Macquarrie,

> involves an element of appropriation. . . . The response of appropriation constitutes, indeed, an essential element in the totality of the revelatory experience. . . . In the

religious experience of revelation, the overwhelmingness of being is matched by its grace, the *tremendum* by the *fascinans,* for being gives itself and opens itself so that we stand in the grace and openness of being. It reveals itself not only in otherness but also in kinship, so that even as we are grasped by it, we can to some extent grasp it in turn and hold to it.[15]

When Macquarrie speaks of revelation and religious knowledge, the knowledge of which he speaks includes perception and intellection within the broader range of our experience as beings in the world, in which no sharp distinctions are drawn between our understanding, feeling, and willing. Existing, not knowing, is the primary category, and within the act of existing in the world our understanding, feeling and willing are together. Thus, this theory of revelation, which views revelatory experience as cognitive, embraces empirical reality inside the larger range of experience. Macquarrie's theory of miracles can help us see this more concretely.

Bultmann in his discussion of miracles had drawn a distinction between the word "miracle" and the word "wonder."[16] Miracle refers to an event which violates the natural order of events and represents God as a supernatural causal agent. Bultmann argues that our modern conception of nature as orderly is well established and cannot be rejected at will. The idea of miracle, according to Bultmann, is a purely intellectual idea and is not essential to religious faith. Even if there were violations of the natural order, there might well be explanations that have nothing to do with religion.

Wonder, not miracle, is, to Bultmann, the proper religious category by which contemporary humankind understands the activity of God. "Wonder" does not refer to an observable event in the world; it is an event hidden from those who do not see God's act in history. The hiddenness of God's act is tied to the belief that knowledge of God is an act of faith. In the religious context, "wonder" refers to the revelation of God, whereby man asks whether he understands the world and himself correctly when he aims at making the world conform to his control and when he defines himself through his work.

Bultmann's discussion of wonder, understood in the context of his emphasis on self-understanding and the otherness of God, is ultimately unsatisfactory, but his pointing to wonder as a revelatory event is an important correction to talking about "miracle" as a violation of the regularity of nature. Macquarrie also rejects the idea of miracle as a supernatural intervention into the order of nature. He argues that this view is irreconcilable with science and history and is a relic of mythological thinking, which expects God to prove himself in some objective way. From a secular point of view, a miracle may be interpreted as an ordinary event, open like all events to secular explanation. But from the point of view of religious faith, such an event may be seen as a vehicle of God's disclosure of himself.

Does this mean then that an ordinary event becomes a miracle only in the subjective experience of the man of faith, or that a miracle is only an ordinary event to which is appended a religious interpretation? Neither of these views is acceptable to Macquarrie. God's presence may be said to be everywhere, but it may be given concentrated expression in particular events, where his presence becomes focused, to use Macquarrie's term. In Biblical events such as crossing the Red Sea, we come up against what Jaspers called a limit situation, in which our ordinary ways of understanding ourselves reach a limit. This prepares us to be open to, or notice in events, dimensions that we might otherwise overlook. However, these dimensions are understood to belong to the events themselves. They are not hidden behind the events or merely added to them. A miracle, in this context, can be understood as

> an interpretive event, in the light of which experience as a whole receives a coherent meaning. The miracle focuses the presence and action that underlies the whole and makes sense of the whole. The miracle is, moreover, not an isolated occasion, for the same presence and the same grace (or judgment) announce themselves in other events. The crossing of the Red Sea was a major focus in the experience of Israel, but around this focus their continuing history was understood in terms of the same divine acting, and their faith was confirmed because at all kinds of lesser foci in the national experience God's presence was known again in grace or judgment, and a total

experience was built up that made sense and strengthened
existence and selfhood and community.[17]

If one understands "miracle" as a revelatory event in
Macquarrie's sense, it is clear that revealed knowledge of God
is interdependent with one's being in the world; it is never a
merely subjective or self-authenticating event. Both the secularist and the person of faith may agree that the Red Sea did not
literally part, and they may both accept, or expect to discover,
an adequate natural explanation of the empirical events. The
religious person differs from the secularist in that he experiences in the event holy Being, which speaks to his quest for
meaning and fulfillment in his existence. Such an experience is
not an isolated event but takes place within the context of his
experience as a whole, including the history of which he is a
part.

Macquarrie's understanding of miracle and the revelation
of God can be put in a more pointed way by looking at his
treatment of the revelation of God in the event of Jesus, which
he says is the supreme miracle for the Christian faith. Macquarrie does not restrict the idea of revelation and knowledge of
God to particular events in history, but he does believe that
historical events combine the existential and ontological dimensions of revelation in a unique way and that the mystery of
Being is focused in a decisive way in the particular historical
being of Jesus the Christ. For Christian faith this revelation is
primordial. It founds the Christian community and deter-
mines its understanding of and comportment to Being or God.

From the secular point of view, Jesus may be approached
as one does any other historical person, with the intent of
understanding who he was. But for the disciples, there was
what we might call a double character to this event, in that
Jesus became for them a particular focus for understanding the
presence and manifestation of Being. It is clear that there was
nothing surrounding the life of Jesus which required awareness of the presence of God. Of those who encountered Jesus,
only a minority looked to him as a focus of the presence and
manifestation of God, and for us it is very difficult to know
even what the publicly observable phenomena were. The diffi-

culties associated with efforts to separate the facts from the mythological and theological accretions are well known. It is almost orthodoxy among New Testament scholars today that the Gospels do not provide us with accounts of Jesus's life but are proclamations of Jesus as the one in whom God has become manifest. The difference between Bultmann's claim that we can know little or nothing about the life of Jesus and the findings of later New Testament scholars is but a matter of degree.

Macquarrie, as we noted in Chapter 1, insists that there is a minimum core of factuality in the story of Jesus. Without it, the revelation of God focused in the event of Jesus the Christ would be no different from other timeless symbols. In all of the controversies about the historical Jesus, the understanding of the general character of Jesus' life has, according to Macquarrie, remained constant.

> To know that he was one who taught that in the face of the end men are called to radical self-giving love, and that he himself lived this way even to the point where he gave himself up to death—this is the essence of the historical Jesus, and it still remains accessible to us. We cannot indeed say that there is certainty here, but there is a high degree of probability, and even the most skeptical researchers have hardly shaken it.[18]

Theologians who overemphasize the infinite qualitative distinction between God and man, the difficulties associated with writing a biography of Jesus, and the role of faith in religious knowledge often tend to shy away from maintaining anything like this minimum core of factuality. In doing so, however, they run the risk of reducing the revelation of God in Christ to a mere ideal and of treating inadequately the question of the justification of religious belief. For Macquarrie, the minimum core of factuality provides an empirical anchor by which the Christian way of life can be affirmed as something that has been realized in history and is therefore to be taken seriously as a possibility for existence. As a paradigm for the understanding of existence, it can stretch our understanding of the possibilities of our being in the world. The life in Christ is a historical symbol of the fulfillment of selfhood. As such it gives testimony to the fullest disclosure of the Being of human existence for those who are open to the deeper dimensions of the publicly observable events of Jesus's life. These events may be said to disclose existence within the wider range of Being itself:

> Jesus Christ may be properly understood as the focus of Being, the particular being in whom the advent and epiphany take place, so that he is taken up into Being itself and we see in him the coming into one of deity and humanity, of creative Being and creaturely being . . . He is definitive in the sense that for Christians he defines in normative fashion both the nature of man (which he has brought to a new level) and the nature of God (for the divine Logos, expressive Being has found its fullest expression in him).[19]

We have examined Macquarrie's understanding of religious knowledge, but have said little about his understanding of argument in relation to religious experience. Macquarrie does not believe religious experience to be universal and self-authenticating, and he admits that the religious interpretation of the experience of the holy is not the only possible one. He believes, however, that the distinctively religious experience cannot be dismissed without good reason and that it warrants serious consideration as *prima facie* evidence for the reality of God.

If one does not have this distinctively religious experience, however, on what grounds can religious and nonreligious persons converse? Macquarrie argues that by showing the interrelationships between religious and other kinds of experience, one can build up reliable patterns that will enable one to make sense of the total range of human experience, help illuminate for others one's own experience, and direct attention to dimensions of experience previously overlooked. Macquarrie's primary emphasis is on describing and interpreting our experience as beings in the world, and he has been hesitant to use the term "argument." In his most recent work, however, he suggests that one can build up from these analyses of experience a cumulative argument which lends support to religious faith.

This argument, which he calls an anthropological argument for the existence of God, is presented in the final chapter of *In Search of Humanity* and builds on the descriptions of the experience of existence and Being outlined in this book. In developing this argument, Macquarrie appeals to an idiom familiar to Western philosophy—of man as a microcosm, a kind of universe in miniature that reflects the character and structure of the macrocosm within which his existence is set. This idiom is consistent with his claim that Being is disclosed in the being of human existence.

Macquarrie believes that a good case can be made for thinking that man in the course of many millions of years has summed up the various stages through which the universe has passed. A human may be understood as a few kilograms of material substances and as such may be said to contain within himself the physical-chemical level of being. A human may also be understood as a living organism assigned a definite place in the animal kingdom. Finally a human may be considered a person, a being endowed with freedom, reason, and conscience. Macquarrie realizes that many theologians, who assert an infinite qualitative difference between God and man would reject the idea that one can proceed from the being of man to God, but he argues that it is at least reasonable to suppose some continuity between human existence and God, on the grounds that Being or God is that without which beings would not be. His claim is that humanity, more than any other form of existence, brings to light the creative forces at work in reality. Although this interpretation of human existence cannot in the strict sense be proven, it can be shown to be reasonable, adequate to the data of experiences of existence and being.

It is on the basis of this affinity between human existence and the wider reality within which it is set that Macquarrie constructs his anthropological argument. Basically, he tries to show that the experience of human existence points toward its fulfillment in transcendent Being, lending credence to the possibility that reality is of the kind attested to in religious experience. Macquarrie does little to help us understand the structure of this argument, except to say that is a cumulative argument and that he is bringing together "considerations drawn from our study of different aspects of human life and cumulatively directing us to a spiritual reality which is at once the source, support and goal of humanity."[20] The expression "cumulative argument" is mentioned one time in the revised version of *Principles of Christian Theology* and then in conjunction with the name Basil Mitchell. In speaking of the cumulative form of argument in his *The Justification of Religious Belief*, Mitchell writes "On this view the theist is urging that traditional Christian theism makes better sense of all the evidence available than does any alternative on offer, and the atheist is contesting this claim." Such an argument, Mitchell suggests, is unlikely to progress unless the various arguments, or series of piecemeal arguments, are brought into relation with one another. "The debate, to be useful, must take the form of a dialogue in which as John Wisdom observes (in relation to a legal judgment), 'The process of argument is not a *chain* of demonstrative reasoning. It is a presenting and representing of those features of a case which severally cooperate in favour of the conclusion'."[21]

Similarly, Macquarrie's anthropological argument for the existence of God can best be understood as an effort to present and represent those patterns of experience which are believed to cooperate in favor of theism. In the strict sense, he does not seem to be arguing for the conclusion that there exists a transcendent being called God. Rather, he seems to be arguing that the most adequate description of the patterns of experience cooperate in favor of the conclusion that reality is gracious or holy and that a theistic interpretation of experience does the most justice to the data. Macquarrie's argument contains six propositions that can be understood as summaries of his descriptions and interpretations of the experience of existence and Being and that are understood by him to direct us to a spiritual reality which is the source, support and goal of humanity.

First, he argues that "human life has brought to light more than anything else that we know astonishing potentialities latent in the physical universe." Adequate interpretations of human existence show it to be more than can be contained in typical nineteenth-century materialistic interpretations of man. Twentieth-century science itself presents us with an understanding of matter as a complex form of energy, calling into question the older reductionist views of man and suggesting unlimited creative forces at work in the universe.

Second, he argues that "some aspects of our humanity suggest a transhuman spiritual source." The higher dimensions of human experience, the intellectual, the moral and the personal suggest that the creative potentialities of the universe trace their origin to a spiritual reality. Language, conscience, and morality all seem to posit a level of being no less personal and spiritual than ourselves. Macquarrie appeals here to the principle of sufficient reason, stated by Leibniz, as one "in virtue of which we hold that there can be no fact real or existing . . . unless there be a sufficient reason why it should be so and not otherwise, although these reasons usually cannot be known by us."[22] Macquarrie argues that even if our understanding is imperfect, these aspects of human existence would seem to point to a spiritual reality that in some sense transcends nature.

Third, "the human being in certain respects transcends nature in such a way as to provide an analogy of divine transcendence and to suggest that the goal of humanity is participation in the life of God." Man's freedom, for example, is more than nature. It is like a breach in nature through which man may be said to be both immanent in the world and transcendent to it. Human freedom, as we indicated earlier in this book, is not without its restraints. It must always be understood within the context of man's facticity. Yet there appears to be an openness in human existence, and an unfinishedness, and related to these a capacity to give creative shape to the world and in particular to human existence itself. Just here, freedom and creativity may be understood to point man beyond the limits of nature and ultimately into a wider reality of freedom and creativity that for the religious person is God. God so understood is not an absolute monarch or an oppressive tyrant, but Creative Being, who in letting-be enables or even encourages man to realize his freedom and creativity.[23]

Fourth "human beings show a natural trust in the wider being within which their existence is set." Although Macquarrie does not single out this proposition from the rest, it is the one that seems particularly fundamental for him. For Macquarrie the sense of confidence in reality as trustworthy distinguishes religious from non-religious commitment. At times, almost in spite of ourselves, we seem to take on commitments that suggest a confidence not only in ourselves and others but also in the basic order of things. And it is this that would seem to provide the basis for hope in the face of suffering and death. This trust or confidence in the face of the ambiguous character of reality is not identical to faith in God, but it does suggest an attitude consistent with faith in God, with an understanding of reality as gracious.[24]

Fifth, "there are some negative factors in human existence which can be understood as limit situations, impressing on us our own finitude and at the same time evoking the idea of absolute being." By "limit situations" Macquarrie refers to experiences such as those analyzed by Jaspers and Tillich that point to human existence as fragmented or limited. Such experiences as death, anxiety, and guilt may be considered negative in that they provoke a dissatisfaction or unease with one's life, an awareness that one is not in full control, and perhaps even a sense that life is absurd. These experiences, however, are not merely negative in import. For Jaspers such experiences open up the possibility of an encounter with Transcendence, in which human existence may realize its freedom from beyond the limits of the observable world. For Tillich, such experiences may provoke fundamental questions of the meaning of human existence to which revelatory experiences may provide answers. Neither Jaspers, Tillich, nor Macquarrie claim a necessary connection between limit, or boundary situations and a recognition of Transcendence or God. Macquarrie argues, however, that such experiences bring us face to face with our own limited being and open us up to the wider range of Being in which we are immersed.

The final proposition in this cumulative argument is that "many of these strands come together in religion in which men and women claim to experience in various ways the reality of God, and this claim has a *prima facie* case for its validity as one deeply rooted in the human condition and one which has never been disproved and perhaps never could be." In the first five propositions Macquarrie is referring to what might be called the transcendent or religious dimensions of ordinary experience, without assigning them any definite religious connotation. In the sixth proposition, however, he is referring to distinctively religious experience, in which the reality of Holy Being or God is understood to impinge on the lives of persons, bringing their existence to fulfillment in encounter with the transcendent other. Such experiences, when described, would seem to require belief in some greater reality or God. Macquarrie is not suggesting that we can appeal to such experiences as proofs of the existence of God, but he does argue that such reports constitute a *prima facie* case for their validity in that they have not been disproved and they appear to be so much a part of the human condition. On these grounds they may be taken as evidence for the reality of God.

What Macquarrie presents as an anthropological argument for the existence of God might be considered by some to be no argument at all. That is, it lacks the rigor of strictly inductive or deductive arguments. Arguments in the humanities, however, do not always conform to strict argument forms. Literary critics, for example, often dispute the interpretation of texts, and appeal to factual data in attempting to settle these disputes. The critic guided by some initial insight attempts to give an account of all data without distorting any of it. The result is a theory which claims to be most adequate to the data. Just so with Macquarrie's anthropological argument for the existence of God. A theistic theory is held to be the most adequate theory in our efforts to give intelligibility to the experience of existence and Being.

Perhaps Macquarrie would agree that in the strict sense he is not trying to answer the question: Does God exist? The question with which he is concerned is closer to "What is Tom like?" than to "Does Tom exist?" We may recall that for Macquarrie, the dispute between atheists and theists is no longer "Does God exist?" but "Is Being Gracious?" In his anthropological argument, Macquarrie is contending that there are dimensions of experience that point toward an understanding of reality that is identified in distinctively religious experience as God. Or, to put it another way, human experience can best be accounted for by reference to reality understood as gracious.

Theologians cannot without risk avoid the task of doing metaphysics, even if many of the past systems have fallen into disarray or been discredited. Macquarrie would have little disagreement with Whitehead's claim that ". . . rational religion must have recourse to metaphysics for a scrutiny of terms. At the same time it [religion] contributes its own independent evidence, which metaphysics must take account of in framing its descriptions."[25] We now turn to a discussion of the role of metaphysics in the meaning and truth of the language of religious faith.

Notes

1. Friedrich Schleiermacher, *The Christian Faith* (Edinburgh: T & T Clark, 1956), pp. 133–34.
2. Martin Buber, *Eclipse of God* (New York: Harper and Row, 1952), p. 28.
3. *Being and Time,* p. 207.
4. I have discussed this in more detail in "Lewis on Experience, Reason and Religious Belief," *The Review of Metaphysics,* xxxv, no. 1, September 1981.
5. Macquarrie, "God in Experience and Argument in," Eugene T. Long, ed., *Experience, Reason and God* (Washington: The Catholic University of America Press, 1980), p. 34.
6. Macquarrie, "Religious Experience," *Humanities,* 12, December 1977, p. 194.
7. *Principles,* p. 8.
8. *Principles,* p. 87.
9. *Principles,* p. 95.
10. The distinction between calculative and meditative thinking is discussed in more detail in my "Being and Thinking," *The Southern Journal of Philosophy,* ix, 1971.
11. *Principles,* pp. 92–93.
12. Martin Heidegger, *Discourse on Thinking* (New York: Harper and Row, 1966), pp. 59–60.
13. Martin Heidegger, *An Introduction to Metaphysics* (New Haven: Yale University Press, 1959), pp. 20ff. See also *Being and Time,* pp. 262ff.; 341ff.
14. Martin Heidegger, *What Is Called Thinking?* (New York: Harper and Row, 1968), pp. 14ff.
15. *Principles,* p. 95.
16. Rudolph Bultmann, *Glauben und Verstehen,* Vol. I (Tubingen: J. C. B. Mohr, 1961), pp. 214ff.
17. *Principles,* p. 253.
18. *Principles,* p. 277.
19. *Principles,* pp. 303–305.
20. *In Search of Humanity,* p. 257.
21. Basil Mitchell, *The Justification of Religious Belief* (London: Macmillan, 1973), pp. 40, 45.
22. Cited by Macquarrie, *In Search of Humanity,* p. 258.
23. *In Search of Humanity,* pp. 11–37.
24. For a related argument which focuses on confidence or trust in

Reality, see Donald Evans, *Faith, Authenticity, and Morality* (Toronto: University of Toronto Press, 1980).

25. Alfred North Whitehead, *Religion in the Making* (New York: Meridan Books, 1960), p. 79. Cited by Bowman Clarke in "Theology and Philosophy," *Journal of the American Academy of Religion,* xxxviii, 3, September 1970. Clarke's understanding of the traditional arguments for the existence of God parallels in some ways Macquarrie's understanding of the anthropological argument.

5

MEANING
AND TRUTH
OF FAITH

SOME EXISTENTIALIST PHILOSOPHERS AND THEOLOGIANS HAVE argued that Christian theism can be neither proven nor shown to be probable in any strict sense, that God is not an object of thought, that there can be no religious *Weltanschauung,* and that one can know and speak of God only out of a relationship to him. Bultmann, for example, argues that we cannot without error speak *about* God, that we can only speak out of a relationship to God in a moment of personal existence. This approach has the value of emphasizing unconditional commitment, which is generally considered to be central to religious faith, but many have argued that it results in a failure both to speak meaningfully of God and to respond adequately to questions concerning the truth of religious faith. Macquarrie is among these critics. He argues that religious faith is a way of being in the world, that it involves understanding as well as commitment, and that it must find expression in some ontology if it is to speak significantly of God.

A parallel development can be seen in the analytical approach to talk of God. Attempts to speak of God within the limits of the verifiability and falsifiability theories of meaning have drawn criticism because those attempts tend to reduce talk of

God to talk of an attitude for which no rational support can be given. Norman Malcolm, in an essay defending one form of the ontological argument for the existence of God, concludes: "At a deeper level I suspect that the argument can be thoroughly understood only by one who has a view of that human 'form of life' that gives rise to the idea of an infinitely great being, who views it from the *inside* not just from the outside and who has, therefore, at least some inclination to *partake* in that religious form of life."[1]

Malcolm is saying that if reason has a role to play in religion, it is connected in some way with a religious form of life. This point has been formulated in a variety of ways by philosophers influenced by Wittgenstein's claim that language is a form of life and by his analysis of the concept "seeing as." According to Wittgenstein, we *see* a table from different perspectives *as*, for example, an object on which to write or *as* a work of art. Seeing, or as some prefer, experiencing, involves interpretation. At times this approach has led to a relativistic form of fideism. However, some philosophers writing within this tradition have argued that we experience the world and ourselves as contingent, that we sense the presence of God as the ground of this contingency, and that reference to transcendent Being is essential to make sense of this experience. Following the suggestion of Wisdom, it is argued that factual disputes are at stake and that one can argue about more and less adequate accounts of the data of experience.

One should not conclude that existentialist and analytical philosophers of religion have arrived at identical positions in their talk of religious faith as a way of being in the world or as a form of life. Even where there are parallels, there are differences in emphasis, the one stressing the experience of language and the other, the logic and syntax of language. There does appear, however, to be something of a convergence of the existential and analytical approaches, and Macquarrie is convinced that progress can be made on the problem of the meaning and truth of religious language only when we understand these two approaches to be complementary.

In his later work Wittgenstein argued that there is no one ideal meaning of language, that there are many meaningful languages, and that the meanings of these languages can be discovered in their uses. For Wittgenstein, this appeal to use implies an appeal to the speaker's existence in the world. That is, the meaning of a sentence is inseparable from the life situations of those who utter it. Here we have, as Macquarrie suggests and as our discussion of discourse in Chapter 1 makes clear, a convergence with Heidegger's existential analysis of language.

As early as *Being and Time,* Heidegger drew the distinction between discourse *(Rede)* and language *(Sprache). Sprache* refers to the actual words and sentences, but *Sprache* is said to have its roots in the existential constitution of man as one who understands himself, or is disclosed to himself in his being in the world. More particularly, *Sprache* has its roots in discourse, where discourse means the disclosure or uncovering of that which is spoken about, letting it show forth itself. Since discourse is bound up with man's disclosure as being in the world, discourse has a kind of being that is worldly, and it is this that comes to expression in the actual words and sentences. Discourse, as Macquarrie suggests, seems to refer to something like an *a priori* structure or what linguists call depth grammar, a potentiality, and *Sprache* refers to something like what linguists call the surface grammar of the actual natural grammar.

For Heidegger, the meaning of language must be understood within the life situations of those beings who are speaking.[2] It is here that we discover the similarities between Heidegger and Wittgenstein of which Macquarrie speaks. Both seem to understand the human situation as the primordial condition for grasping the meaning of language. But whereas Wittgenstein and his followers concentrate on the rules that govern the use of language, Heidegger has given more attention to an analysis of the discourse situation, that is, to the content of the life and experiences of those beings who use the language. For Macquarrie, who is primarily under the influence of Heidegger and who is primarily interested in the language of religion, this means that we need to understand religious language within the experiences of the community of faith.

Macquarrie's analysis of the language of religion begins with the discourse situation, in which language is understood within the context of one's being in the world. It is important to keep this in mind in reading Macquarrie because isolated passages may suggest that language expresses a private thought and refers to experience in a subjective sense.[3] More typically, however, language is understood within the dialectic of man's being in the world, and because of this he shares something with John Smith, who defines experience as an encounter in order to emphasize that we confront something already there.[4] According to Macquarrie, the meaning of language is discovered neither in private mental events nor in descriptive reports of behavior. The meaning of language is discovered in what is disclosed or brought to light in the total discourse situation. The discourse situation, following Heidegger, is said to be composed of three interrelated factors: the speaker, the persons spoken to, and that about which we speak. And language (*Sprache*) brings these together.

In speaking, the speaker is said to *express* himself, and since the self is always already being in the world—that is, bound up and occupied with the world—expression is always of self and world together. Presumably in all cases, speaking expresses one's existence in the world and is self-involving. Such expressions, however, may be more or less complete. Speaking may express more or less fully man's being in the world. In scientific language, for example, the personal dimension of man's being in the world is so dimmed as to be almost eliminated, whereas in the languages of history, poetry, and theology we approach a fuller understanding of human existence. In the language of some analytical philosophers, it might be said that all language has elements of self-involvement and reference but that the degree of self-involvement differs, depending on the use to which language is being put.

Language, then, gives expression to the self and world in varying degrees of adequacy. But how is language related to the subject under discussion? Macquarrie says that language *refers* to its subject matter or that the subject matter is represented in it. This representation, however, has to be understood within the total discourse situation. Macquarrie does not use reference or representation as restrictively as they are used in either the picture or ideational theories of meaning, wherein, the meaning of an expression is limited to the fact or idea represented. For Macquarrie, language refers or represents by providing symbols that refer in different ways, depending on the context in which the language is spoken. For example, this referring may on some occasions be more direct and on other occasions more indirect. Further, just as there are different modes of discourse (for example, scientific, poetic, theological), there must be different modes of referring or representing. In every case, however, discourse must refer to some content beyond itself, and language is the means whereby this content is made accessible to the understanding in order that we might relate to it and find our way about the world in some intelligible sense.

Discourse, then, is giving expression to one's existence in the world. It is also reference and representation in that some content is articulated and given shape. And it is communication, for through language a speaker expresses himself as a being in the world in the context of other beings in the world. Speaker and hearer share a world in common, and communication occurs when some aspect of this world is articulated and made accessible to both parties. Meaning and understanding, then, seem to depend on this shared world of speaker and hearer and should be distinguished from merely emotive or private experiences. Macquarrie summarizes it in this way:

> Discourse is meaningful if it succeeds in lighting up and making accessible to the understanding that which is talked about. Expression, representation and communication would all seem to be essential to meaningful discourse. If nothing is expressed or represented, nothing is brought to light. And even if something is expressed and represented, the discourse breaks down and is unmeaning to the person to whom it is addressed if it fails to communicate.[5]

Two more points must be made if we are to fill out the discourse situation, as Macquarrie understands it. It has already been suggested that something's being meaningful, or understood, is ultimately dependent on its being articulated in language. However, Macquarrie believes that this act of articulation presupposes a more fundamental relation, the relation of language to what is talked about. And that relation is dependent on an openness, or awareness, similar to Kant's *Anschauung*, except that for Macquarrie this awareness is not restricted to those sensuous intuitions on which our perceptions of objects depend. Apart from language, intuition would remain blind or inarticulate. It is because of this awareness, or openness, in his being in the world that man has anything to articulate, and this awareness may include what Heidegger has called affective states or moods, such as anxiety as well as sensuous intuitions. These affective states may also uncover or disclose our existence in the world, making accessible structures that can be articulated in language. According to Macquarrie and Heidegger, the content of these affective states is non-objectifiable since they have to do with total existence and embrace both subject and object. This non-objectifiable content, as will be seen, creates particular problems for the task of articulation in language.

In addition to this openness to one's being in the world, discourse is said also to presuppose a person-to-person relation that makes communication possible. This relation, as Macquarrie understands it, is more primordial than a relation that implies language. It is a relation at the level of inarticulate feeling, yet genuinely personal. He finds support for this primordial relation in this remark by Heidegger: "In discourse, Being-with (*Mitsein*) becomes 'explicitly' *shared*; that is to say, it *is* already, but it is unshared as something that has not been taken hold of and appropriated."[6] Macquarrie finds support too in Josiah Royce's statement that interpretation implies a community of interpretation and that the loyalty or fidelity of its members makes this community possible.[7] Language, then, is said to have its meaning in the discourse situation, defined earlier as composed of the interrelations between speaker, the persons spoken to, and that which gets spoken about. Language functions to unite these three and to disclose and articulate what would otherwise remain hidden. This relationship and disclosure presupposes human existence, with its fundamental awareness or openness to its own being in the world as well as to other centers of existence in the world.

Given this general existential analysis of language and discourse, we now turn to the more particular problem of the language of religion. Language is said to have its significance in the discourse situation, in the life and experiences of those who use language. In the case of religious language, this means that we must understand it, says Macquarrie, from within the "experiences of the community of faith, in which men move from the questioning of their own being to the search for meaning and to the revelatory experience in which they are grasped by the grace of Being. The language in which they express this has its intelligible logic in the pattern of experience through which they move."[8]

In religious language, the speaker is said to express faith, where faith is not merely intellectual assent to doctrines but an existential attitude of acceptance and commitment in the face of Being as gracious. Religious faith is neither a non-cognitive attitude nor an attitude that can be reduced to scientific propositions or propositions that express an intention to act in a particular way. Faith is an existential attitude involving both discernment and commitment. It expresses an attitude of acceptance and commitment which is inseparable from what are believed to be insights into the way things are.[9] Faith is inseparable from a view in which man looks beyond himself and discovers in the grace of Being a meaning for existence that is given from beyond his own resources. This insight into the way things are differs from the views of Sartre and Camus in which existence and Being are experienced as absurd or meaningless. In contrast, religious faith is understood to express a discernment of the meaningfulness of existence and a commitment to God or Being understood as gracious as the ground of this discernment. For Macquarrie, attitudes and moods occur within the context of man's being in the world. They are not merely subjective and may be said to be appropriate or not appropriate in relation to the conditions that prevail.[10] Religious faith is neither unavoidable nor compatible with all states of affairs. For example, it might be falsified by the presence of massive, senseless, and irremediable evil, although Macquarrie admits that it may be impossible to say precisely what such a state of affairs would entail.[11] What is at stake here is not belief in this or that particular theological proposition but the primary discernment upon which all particular theological propositions stand or fall. Similarly, John Baillie has suggested that the question at hand is not analogous to asking what would make one reverse a particular judgment of sense perception, but rather to asking what would lead one to distrust sense perception as a whole and consequently surrender belief in the reality of the corporeal world.[12] Presumably, religious belief would be lost only if the primary discernment were lost—if, for example, one found oneself no longer able to discover a transcendent source of meaning in events where one had found it in the past. The possibility that existence and Being be discerned as meaningful or as absurd must be real if the commitment to Being as gracious is to be meaningful or reasonable in any significant sense.

The language of religion gives expression to the believer's understanding of his existence in the world and to Being understood as gracious, which is the ground of this self-understanding. The language of religion gives expression to faith, where faith refers to an attitude of the self in which the self is directed toward Being understood as the source of meaning within existence. However, Macquarrie wishes to escape the cul de sac of those existentialist theories of religious language that translate all theological assertions into assertions about human existence. Faith is intentional as well as existential, meaning that theological assertions must have a referential dimension that is not reducible to self-understanding.[13] Language must in some way refer to Being understood as gracious. How does this take place?

On the one hand, it is clear that assertions about Being cannot refer to or picture Being in the same way that assertions may be said to refer to or picture empirical facts or beings. Being is transcendent to beings. On the other hand, assertions about Being cannot be properly understood as totally other than assertions about beings. This is the error of negative theology, which then has to accept the consequence that it has nothing significant to say about Being.[14] Macquarrie, like Heidegger, understands Being to manifest itself in relation to beings and to disclose beings as beings.

In completing this analysis of the discourse situation, we have to consider the viewpoint of the person to whom something is said. From the listener's point of view, the language of religion may be said to communicate or share the understanding of Being that has been appropriated in faith. This communicating, or sharing, presupposes a common frame of reference between speaker and listener that Macquarrie finds in the language of existence and Being. This is not to say that people are universally religious or that only religious people can understand what the religious believer is saying. It is to say that men and women share an understanding of existence and Being and that unless the believer can relate what is to be said to what is already understood, even if *pre-thematically*, there would remain an unbridgeable gap of incomprehension. If, for example, one is able to understand the meaning of an ancient love poem, one must have some understanding of love gained from one's own experience. This does not mean that my understanding of love must be identical to that of the poem or that I can comprehend nothing beyond the limits of my present personal experience. It does mean that there must be some parallel between my understanding of love and the understanding of love in the poem if I am to understand it. These two expressions of love may then be grasped as parallel ones that may shed light on each other. Macquarrie quotes Dilthey approvingly when the latter writes: "Interpretation would be impossible if expressions of life were completely strange. It would be unnecessary if nothing strange were in them. It lies, therefore, between these two extremes."[15]

Communication between persons ultimately looks to parallel modes of expression, or parallel languages. One language sheds light on the other, bringing out its meaning, which in turn sheds light on the other language. In the case of theological language, this means that the concrete symbolic language of religion ultimately looks to a more conceptual language of existence and Being, in relation to which the language of the community of faith may be understood. And as the language of faith may shed light on this more universal language of existence and Being, so the latter may shed light on the former.[16]

According to Macquarrie, then, the language of religion gives expression to religious faith, where faith refers simultaneously to a discernment, or insight, into the way things are, to Being understood as gracious and as the source of meaning within existence, and to an attitude of commitment to Being understood as gracious. The communication of this discernment and commitment is said to be contingent on shared experience, and the structure of language, which refers to Being, is said to be symbolic and analogical. Assertions about Being refer to beings, but language about beings is stretched, or qualified, so that it obliquely refers to the presence of Being in the disclosure of beings as beings. Religious and theological language refer symbolically and analogically to God as the ground of beings that are, to God's disclosure of himself, as that which enables beings to be. We need to examine in greater detail the way we use language to make these oblique references.

Like a number of other contemporary theologians and philosophers of religion, Macquarrie, as we recall from Chapter 1, draws distinctions between the terms "myth," "symbol," and "analogy" and between mythological, symbolic, and analogical modes of interpreting language. "Myth," generally defined, refers to a dramatic narrative in which supernatural agencies are at work and in which events and persons are not always subject to considerations of space and time. A myth is said to be interpreted mythologically when no clear distinction is made between the literal and figurative meanings in myth. This does not mean that mythological interpretations of myths are reduced to the merely literal understanding of myths but that no clear distinction is made between what is literal and what is not. While it is likely that ancient man understood the events referred to in myths in a literal sense, he probably also grasped what we might call the figurative or symbolic meanings of myths.

Some people, of course, may still fail to draw a distinction between the literal and figurative meanings of myths. For most people, however this is no longer a reasonable alternative. Assuming that we concern ourselves at all with myths, we probably attempt to understand their figurative or symbolic meanings. In this case we are conscious of the figurative meanings of myths, and the language we use to express this interpretation may be called symbolic.

The word "symbol" is problematic. In the broadest sense a symbol is anything that represents or stands for something else. Macquarrie, following a distinction made by Edwyn Bevan between a symbol that does not convey knowledge about what is symbolized and a symbol that does, speaks of conventional and intrinsic symbols. Mathematical and logical symbols are arbitrary conventions. A more problematic conventional symbol might be "red ribbon" in this sentence: "A red ribbon is a symbol that he is a visitor." In these examples there does not seem to be any intrinsic relation between the symbol and what is symbolized. Such symbols are mere conventions, what Tillich called signs. In the case of an intrinsic symbol, however, there seems to be an intrinsic connection between the symbol and what it symbolizes. Dove, for example, seems to be more than an arbitrary convention in "the dove is a symbol of the peace movement." Granted that such symbols may have been mere conventions at one time, they have developed historical associations, which make them informative and distinguish them from mere arbitrary conventions.

In religious language, the primary concern is with such intrinsic symbols as the cross, the wheel, water, and light. Macquarrie distinguishes between intrinsic symbols that have universal application and are essentially self-interpreting and those that depend on the history of a particular community and require knowledge of that community to be understood. In the Christian community, for example, the cross is a symbol of God's love because of its association with the crucifixion of Jesus. Apart from knowledge of its association with Jesus and the faith of the Christian community, the cross would not be understood in this manner. In fact, the cross served as a symbol of immortality in ancient Egypt, and of fertility in Central America. The symbolic meaning of the cross seems to depend on its associations with particular communities. By contrast, water as a symbol has more universal application and almost always represents cleansing.

Religious symbols then vary considerably with regard to the universality of their application. Some symbols have a very narrow application and depend on associations with a particular historical community. Others seem to transcend particular historical associations and have more universal applications. Religious symbols operate like metaphors in that they may sharpen our understanding, and may draw our attention to some feature of a situation that we otherwise might not have noticed. However, the religious symbol has another characteristic; it calls for a response, a commitment. In the Christian community the meaning of the cross is not limited to the discernment of a love that surpasses human love. It is also understood to summon believers to commit themselves to that way of being. Symbols understood in this sense depend on a background of shared ideas and experiences and remain symbols only as long as they continue to disclose what they symbolize and relate it to our understanding of human existence.

The importance of symbolic language in religion is that it is capable of evoking discernment and commitment, a response that goes beyond mere intellectual assent to a set of propositions. Symbols may disclose levels of meaning that conceptual language fails to reveal. According to Macquarrie, however, religious symbols do not merely evoke non-cognitive feeling in the face of an unknown. They convey insight into the nature of what is symbolized. For this reason, Macquarrie rejects the tendency of some Roman Catholic thinkers to view symbolic language as merely subjective and prefers to talk of the existential connotation of symbols rather than of their subjective aspect. [17]

He also argues, however, that symbolic language is inadequate as a reflective language of religion. Symbols may disclose levels of meaning that go beyond conceptual language, but without the conceptual elucidation of symbolic meaning, symbolic meaning lapses into obscurity. Thus, although symbolic language is essential in providing a concrete vehicle for understanding that surpasses the merely conceptual, a more conceptual language is needed to amplify the meaning of the symbolic language. This Macquarrie finds in analogical language. Symbolic and analogical language shed light on each other. Analogical language provides a more conceptual understanding of the meaning of religious symbols, and symbolic language illuminates the existential character of the analogical utterances.

According to Macquarrie, then, an analogue is more conceptual in character than a symbol. Furthermore, the best analogies are universal, or essentially self-interpreting; they depend less on the background of a particular community for explanation. Finally, an analogy depends on some likeness or affinity between the analogue and that for which it stands. What do we mean by a likeness between the analogue and the analogate?

When one uses such analogues as love to speak of God, it is clear that the analogue is not like God in being identical to or in picturing God. Tillich, attempting to avoid the associations of identity and picturing, refers to participation. A symbol is said to participate in the reality and meaning of that to which it points in the sense that an individual participates in a community. Macquarrie uses such words as "kinship" and "affinity" to speak of the relationship between the analogue and that to which it refers, and he says he has in mind the kind of relationship that exists between a person and his language. Language is not *like* the speaker, but it does in some sense disclose or reveal the speaker. "The language expresses the man; alternatively, he expresses *himself* in his language." [18] John Smith has something similar in mind when he speaks of persons as centers of intentions who "discover each other as persons through experiential encounters mediated by signs or language."[19] Persons express themselves in their signs, symbols, and actions. Without these it would be impossible for us to know each other. Yet persons are not identical to their behavior; they in some sense transcend it. Thus, we are directed by signs, symbols, and behavior to the experiential situation in which a person is disclosed to us in his behavior while also transcending it.

Similarly, the language of analogy in religion refers to an experiential foundation, to a situation in which God discloses or expresses himself as in the world and as transcending the world. In the cases of man's expression of himself and God's expression of himself, we are directed not merely to the words spoken but to the situation in which the words are spoken. And just as the words do not express man as he is in himself but man as he is related or known to the listener, so the so-called Word of God expresses not God as he is in himself but God as he is disclosed to one who hears his Word. The words and actions which mediate our relation to God, which give insight into the nature of God as he is for us, are related to God in the way that the words and actions of a person are related to him when he reveals himself to us. Analogues express or give insight into the nature of God, but God is not identical with these expressions.

According to Macquarrie, the key to understanding this relationship between language and God is the assertion that God is to be understood as Being rather than a being. Traditionally, and particularly among Protestant thinkers, there has been a tendency to assert an analogy between God and beings, based on a view of God as a kind of super-being who differs from other beings only in being the cause of his own being. This analogy between God and beings resulted in a tendency to lose the transcendence of God. It was against this view that the twentieth-century theologian Karl Barth spoke in his earlier work, asserting the infinite qualitative distinction between God and man. In this case, however, the possibility of analogies between God and beings was eliminated, with the result that nothing significant could be said of God.

In asserting that God is to be understood as Being, Macquarrie believes that he is able to avoid both of these errors and make possible an *analogia entis* consistent with the theological understanding of God as transcendent and in the world. In seeking a clarification of the meaning of Being, he turns to Heidegger. According to Heidegger, as was indicated earlier, Being is the transcendens, the incomparable, and is "wholly other" in relation to any particular being. At the same time, Being is said to be inseparable from beings. It is the transcendens without which beings would not be. Being is manifest in beings, and apart from them the word "Being" would be empty of meaning.

Since Being is incomparable with particular beings, it cannot be said that any particular property of a being is identical with Being. Nevertheless, Being is the condition that there are any beings or properties of beings at all. Because of this, Macquarrie argues that it is more appropriate to attribute the positive characteristics of beings to Being or God than the contrary. However, since God or Being is also the transcendens, these properties are not applied to Being in a literal way. They are applied in an oblique way, which we indicate by adding such qualifiers as "infinitely" and "all." God is said to be "infinitely good" and "all wise."

Macquarrie makes the same point in saying that all symbolic and analogical language has a paradoxical character. To avoid the kind of literalness that identifies some aspect of the world with God, he says,

> whatever symbol or analogue is affirmed must be at the same time denied; or, better still, whenever one symbol is affirmed, others that will modify and correct it must be affirmed at the same time. Thus the New Testament, in trying to explicate the person of Christ, applied to him a number of images—'Son of Man,' 'Son of God,' 'Messiah,' 'Lord,' 'Word.' It is impossible to 'harmonize' all these ideas, but out of agreements and conflicts something of the mystery of the incarnation finds expression."[20]

Macquarrie's theory of analogy is close to what has traditionally been called the analogy of attribution, in which one of the analogates is said to possess the characteristics predicated of it in a formal, that is, univocal, sense and the other analogate is said to possess the characteristics predicated of it in a derivative sense. To use Frederick Ferre's example, the word "healthy" may apply to man in a formal sense and to mountain resorts that enable man to be healthy in a derivative sense.[21] In a similar way, Macquarrie might say that goodness applies to man in a formal sense but to God in a derivative sense, in that God is the condition that lets be or enables goodness in man. In saying that analogies for God are paradoxical in character, however, Macquarrie intends to preserve the sense of the incomparable in God. The constellation of analogues used gives insight into the incomparable nature of God.

One of the difficulties traditionally associated with this theory of analogy is that it is overly permissive. If God enables all beings and qualities to be, then it would seem that one should attribute to God all conceivable properties in the derivative sense. Although any word may become an analogy of God and the disclosure of Being may be possible at any time or place, Macquarrie says that there are particular historical disclosures of God and that the symbols of these disclosures are not arbitrarily chosen but "are given by Being which has addressed us in and through them. The great symbols and analogues of the Christian religion, for instance, the cross, the fatherhood of God, and the suffering servant, have their depth of meaning only in the context of this particular revelation of God, and they cohere together in a constellation, as it were, each shedding light on the other."[22]

Macquarrie's point is similar to Ian Crombie's when the latter argues that we accept the images we employ on authority.[23] In his philosophical theology, however, Macquarrie is concerned that the symbols and analogues cohere not only with the experience and beliefs of the community of faith but also with our general beliefs about the nature of reality. For this reason, he argues that some entities are more adequate than others to the disclosure and understanding of God. Those entities most adequate in lighting up or disclosing God are those whose affinities with Being are of the widest range. For example, symbols and analogies drawn from the life of man, an entity who combines the characteristics of material being, animal organism, and personal being, are more adequate than symbols drawn from mere material objects. Whereas mere material beings simply *are,* personal beings, with their characteristics of freedom and creativity, *let be* and thus may be the basis for the understanding of Being as letting-be. Generally speaking, then, personal language is held to be more adequate than non-personal language for discourse about Being and God.

According to Macquarrie, the language of religion refers to Being or God as it is known in revelatory experience. Thus, while theological language might ostensibly point to some particular being, its meaning is properly grasped only when it is seen to open a way into the disclosure of Being. Just as a well chosen metaphor may bring to our attention some feature of a situation that we otherwise might have overlooked, so theological language draws our attention to the presence of Being that lies hidden in our ordinary chatter about the world. Our saying that the language of a person is ultimately appropriated only in our experience of the speaker's disclosure of himself is analogous to saying that the meaning of theological language is ultimately appropriated only in our experience of the disclosure of Being. We recall, however, that Macquarrie does not limit understanding of God to the experience of faith. He appeals to the more universal language of existence and Being as a way of illuminating the language of religious faith.

According to Macquarrie, the relation between the "concrete" symbolic language of the Christian religion and the more conceptual analogical language of existence and Being is dialectical. "The particular symbols are illuminated by the language of existence and being, but these concrete symbols become in turn illuminating for relatively abstract statements of an existential or ontological character.[24] Symbolic language thus lights up levels of meaning that more conceptual language cannot express. But without the conceptual elucidation of symbolic meaning, which we discover in analogical language, the symbolic meaning would lapse into obscurity.[25] In moving from symbolic language to analogical language, we are not moving from symbolic to literal language in the strict sense. We are moving from "symbols having a greater measure of particularity, in the sense that they belong within a limited historical community, to symbols which come nearer to a universality of intelligibility."[26] Symbolic language may be said to evoke an awareness of the presence of God more than it describes God, and it stands in need of rational interpretation in more conceptual language. Neither symbolic

(98)

nor analogical language can be taken literally, according to Macquarrie, but each sheds light on the other leading dialectically to the unhiddenness or uncovering of God.

Religious faith, as we have seen, is an attitude of trust and commitment. It is not, however, a merely subjective attitude or blik. Faith is intentional in structure in that it refers to God or Being understood as gracious, the ground of its trust and commitment. The language of religion is understood to have a structure of self-involvement and intentionality, and theology has to develop intelligible concepts for articulating its subject matter and for enabling one to make judgments as to the truth of religion. This brings us to the point at which we began this chapter. According to Macquarrie, religious faith is a matter of unconditional commitment, but unlike some existential and analytical philosophers, Macquarrie does not conclude that religious faith is self-authenticating or that there can be no religious *Weltanschauung*. He speaks of religious faith as a way of being in the world, but he does not believe that the religious form of life is simply one option among others, one for which no rational criteria can be given. And although he appeals to religious experience, he is critical of those who attempt to establish the validity of religious belief merely on descriptions of religious experience. Macquarrie remains essentially a phenomenologist, but he does not ignore the question of truth.

How then does Macquarrie address the question of truth in religion? We turn once more to Heidegger, who defines truth as uncovering or disclosing. Heidegger objects to *defining* truth as correspondence between knower and known but does not rule out correspondence as a *criterion* of truth. Heidegger is concerned with the foundation for the claim that a statement is true if it corresponds to things as they are. Things, he argues, must show themselves as they are and true judgments do not determine things as they are but render things accessible to us, bring us into the immediate presence of things. Truth is an uncovering or disclosing of what is, and man is said to be in the truth to the extent that he is open to things as they are, to the extent that he lets things be. Once again, letting be is not an attitude of indifference to things but a struggle of the will to avoid determining and manipulating things, an approach to things that attempts to remove the obstacles in order that things might be seen as they are. Language may be said to be true or false to the extent that it uncovers or conceals that to which it refers.

Macquarrie's theory of the truth of religious language is dependent on Heidegger's definition of truth. The language of religion, according to Macquarrie, may be said to be true to the extent that it lights up or discloses reality as it is given. No statement can fully disclose existence and Being, and, because of this, Macquarrie accepts the Bradlian notion of degrees of truth. Symbolic and analogical statements are combined to illuminate, to let be shown the total range of the experience of existence and Being. Religious statements, then, cannot be held to be true in and of themselves. They must cohere with other religious statements and ultimately with statements expressing our secular beliefs if they are to be adequate to the disclosure of reality as a whole. Macquarrie writes that "although phenomenology does not offer proof or demonstration, its truth-claim is nevertheless open to testing. The test is to compare the description offered with our own first-hand understanding of existence, i.e., to confront the phenomenological account with the phenomena themselves as we have access to them."[28] Elsewhere he suggests that the criterion for religious statements is some form of phenomenology and agrees with Tillich that

> Theology must apply the phenomenological approach to all its basic concepts, forcing its critics first of all to see what the criticized concepts mean and also forcing itself to make careful descriptions of its concepts and to use them with logical consistency. . . . The test of a phenomenological description is that the picture given by it be convincing, that it can be seen by anyone who is looking in the same direction, that the description illuminates related ideas, and that it makes the reality which these ideas are supposed to reflect understandable.[20]

Macquarrie has not fully developed the implications of such statements about the nature and criteria of truth, but some points emerge clearly. He rejects the idea that the language of religion can be shown to be true by way of strict deductive and inductive arguments. Faith and understanding arise from interpreting experiences, not from inferring from experiences.

He also rejects approaches which argue that religion makes no claims that are subject to questions of truth and falsity, as well as those approaches which appeal to self-authentication as the only mode of truth applicable to religous assertions. His position is closer to those who argue that what is at stake is a shift in ways of experiencing or interpreting the same data. Even here, however, Macquarrie has reservations, for he wants to avoid any position that would lead to conceptual relativism. The difference between the atheistic and the theistic interpretations of existence and Being is not for him merely a matter of different presuppositions or changing *Gestalten*.

Heidegger's position, as I have argued elsewhere, leaves us with an inadequate development of criteria for evaluating beliefs about Being, and Macquarrie also seems to express some dissatisfaction with Heidegger on this point.[30] Macquarrie seems to be moving beyond Heidegger and toward the view developed by Dorothy Emmett, Whitehead, and others with regard to the nature of metaphysical thinking. Macquarrie suggests that the theist begins with an experience or perspective, that this perspective is amplified into a set of theistic assertions and ultimately into an ontological theory designed to describe, or give an account of, the total range of the experience of existence and Being. Macquarrie has, in fact, expressed appreciation for the methodologies of such persons as Whitehead and Alexander while criticizing their conclusions. He cites in particular their keeping in close touch with experience and the natural sciences, their avoidance of the extremes of idealism, and their effort to give consideration to the varied aspects of experience.[31]

Macquarrie hesitates to use the word "metaphysics," partly because the term frequently refers to attempts to grasp reality in rational terms and partly because Macquarrie believes that metaphysics has traditionally misconceived God as a being. Nevertheless, he shares much in common with those who argue that religious faith issues in a world view or a metaphysical theory that may be judged true or false in accordance with its capacity to make sense of human experience. A metaphysical theory may be judged true to the extent that the various elements can be shown to be consistent with each other and to the extent that the theory gives an adequate account of the total range of the experience of existence and Being.

Heidegger's "metaphysics," or fundamental ontology, is judged by Macquarrie to be the most adequate secular description of the experience of existence and Being. It is also appropriate to interpreting and explaining the Christian faith in more universal terms. Heidegger's analysis of existence and Being can be used to help shed light on the religious way of life and its understanding of reality as meaningful and self-giving. If Heidegger may be said to provide for Macquarrie the essentials of a method and a language by which to speak significantly of God, theology provides a vision, an insight into dimensions of experience that must be taken into account by any ontological theory. And it is in the dialectic between Christian theology and Heidegger's ontology that expression may be given to that form of life which is judged to be most adequate to the total range of human experience.

In his discussion of the truth of faith, Macquarrie, like other phenomenologists, seems for the most part to rely on describing and on appealing to others to see the phenomena as he sees them. Even here, however, there seems to be a place for argument. Heidegger for example seems at times to be saying: "You are aware of this phenomenon. You have interpreted it in this manner. But now look at it in this manner. Doesn't this make more sense of the phenomenon?" Yet Macquarrie seems somewhat uneasy with this approach, and rightly so. He wants to be able not only to describe but also to explain and to argue that this or that ontological theory gives a more adequate account of the experience of existence and Being than the available alternatives. Without this, it is difficult to see how the illumination associated with metaphysics differs from psychological illumination in literature.

Much of Macquarrie's discussion of the truth of faith depends on Heidegger's theory of truth, but this leads to some difficulties since Heideggers' theory is at times obscure and he has done little to clarify the criteria of truth. Heidegger has distinguished his definition of truth from the Platonic-Aristotelian-Medieval definition, arguing that the modern correspondence definition of truth finds its prototype in Plato. C. B. Daly, however, has argued that the idea of truth in Plato, which through Augustine and Aquinas emerged as the doctrine of truth as adequacy, is different from some modern correspondence notions of truth and is close to Heidegger's own position. In one essay Macquarrie seems to accept this reading of Heidegger. After suggesting that St. Thomas's definition of truth be understood as "adequacy" rather than correspondence, Macquarrie explains that "what we say is true to the extent that it is adequate to what we are talking about, that is to say, to the extent to which it is able to light up what is talked about, so that we see it for what it is."[32]

If one were to develop Macquarrie's notion of truth in the direction of truth as adequacy, one might be able to say that theological statements are true to the extent that they cohere with other theological and non-theological statements in a metaphysical theory that provides the most adequate explanation of the whole range of experience. Such a theory would have to be adequate to the data of the empirical sciences, but it would also have to explain those transcendent dimensions within experience that are not accounted for in theories limited to what is verifiable by observational tests. This procedure would not seek to make experience fit an existing theory or language. It would seek a language and a theory adequate to experience.[33]

This approach need not result in the assimilation of religious faith to metaphysical theory. Religious language looks to metaphysical language in an effort to illuminate and justify religious assertions. Ultimately, however, the religious form of life is not merely a matter of making true assertions, as Macquarrie's theory makes clear. The language of faith is also a language of self-involvement, in which one expresses a new self-understanding in relation to the actual presence of divine reality. The anchorage of religious language is the experience of the presence of the divine, and a metaphysical theory adequate to this experience must point to the symbolic language of religion, which opens up the possibility of experiencing in certain ambiguous events the presence of God.

Notes

1. Norman Malcolm. "Anselm's Ontological Arguments," *The Existence of God*, ed., John Hick (London: Collier-Macmillan, 1969), p. 67.
2. See my article "Language and Meaning in Heidegger's *Being and Time*," *Proceedings of the XVth World Congress of Philosophy* (Sofia, 1973).
3. Walter Biemel has defended Heidegger against a similar misunderstanding. See Biemel, "Poetry and Language in Heidegger," *On Heidegger and Language*, ed., Joseph J. Kockelmans (Evanston: Northwestern University Press, 1972), pp. 69ff.
4. John Smith, *Experience and God* (New York: Oxford, 1968), pp. 21ff.
5. *God-Talk*, p. 75.
6. *Being and Time*, p. 205. See *God-Talk*, p. 77.
7. *God-Talk*, pp. 77–78.
8. *Principles*, p. 125.
9. Macquarrie has pointed out the parallel between his approach and that of Ian Ramsey, where the latter talks about discernment and commitment: *Principles*, p. 127. Macquarrie is sympathetic with Braithwaite's efforts at showing the relation between religious language and conduct but criticizes him for ignoring the sense in which religion can also be said to give insight into the kind of world in which one acts. Macquarrie is probably closer to Wisdom, who speaks of the religious believer as one who notices certain patterns in experience. However, Macquarrie wants to avoid the tendency toward relativism in Wisdom's position. See John Macquarrie, *Twentieth-Century Religious Thought: The Frontiers of Philosophy and Theology, 1900–1980* (New York: Charles Scribner's Sons, 1981), p. 316.
10. *Existentialism*, pp. 118ff.
11. *Principles*, p. 102. For the theist, the experience of evil is relative to the experience of the absolute goodness of God and presumably remains less than absolute so long as God is believed to exist. Macquarrie seems to be saying that theism is rooted in a perspective or a set of assumptions within which ambiguous events are interpreted and understood, but that these assumptions are open to analysis and criticism, the result of which may be alteration or even rejection.

12. John Baillie, *The Sense of the Presence of God* (London: Oxford University Press, 1962), p. 72.
13. *Thinking About God*, p. 11. I have discussed this difficulty in the existentialist theory of religious language in *Jaspers and Bultmann: A Dialogue Between Philosophy and Theology in the Existentialist Tradition* (Durham: Duke University Press, 1968), pp. 79ff.
14. See my essay "Jaspers' Philosophy of Existence as a Model for Theological Reflection," *International Journal for Philosophy of Religion*, Vol. III, No. 1, 1972, 35ff.
15. *Principles*, p. 37. W. Dilthey, *Meaning In History*, ed., H. P. Rickman (London: George Allen and Unwin, 1961), p. 77.
16. *Principles*, p. 37–38, 130. *God-Talk*, pp. 74ff.
17. *God-Talk*, pp. 216ff.
18. God-Talk, p. 220.
19. John Smith, *The Analogy of Experience* (New York: Harper and Row, 1973), p. 95.
20. *God-Talk*, p. 228. See also *Principles*, p. 145.
21. Frederick Ferre, *Language, Logic and God* (New York: Harper and Brothers, 1961), p. 73.
22. *Principles*, p. 143.
23. I. M. Crombie, "Arising from the University Discussion," *New Essays in Philosophical Theology* (London: SCM Press, 1955), p. 124.
24. *Principles*, p. 137.
25. *God-Talk*, 201–202.
26. *God-Talk*, p. 239. The problems associated with defining literal language as opposed to metaphorical language are many and Macquarrie has not addressed them in detail. He would say, I believe, that literal language is language used in a "straightforward" way. That is, the meaning of a literal utterance is its surface meaning, that meaning which conforms to the ordinary use of terms and is essentially self-interpreting and universally understood. Symbolic and analogical utterances may be understood as in some sense descriptive and subject to questions of truth and falsity. However, this language refers indirectly, and meaning is dependent on interpretation and explanation. See *God-Talk*, p. 114ff.
27. *Being and Time*, pp. 256ff. Heidegger, "On the Essence of Truth," *Existence and Being*, ed., Werner Brock (Chicago: Henry Regnery, 1967), pp. 292–324.
28. *Existentialsm*, p. 12.

29. *Studies,* pp. 40–41.
30. "Being and Thinking," *The Southern Journal of Philosophy,* 9 (Summer 1971), 138ff. See *Thinking About God,* pp. 15ff.
31. *Twentieth-Century Religious Thought,* pp. 276–77.
32. *Thinking About God,* pp. 23–24. C. B. Daly, "Metaphysics and the Limits of Language," *Prospect for Metaphysics,* ed., Ian Ramsey (London: Allen and Unwin, 1961), pp. 200–203.
33. For an elaboration of this approach see my "Experience and the Justification of Religious Belief," *Religious Studies,* 17, pp. 499–510.

A Chronological List of the Works of John Macquarrie

"Feeling and Understanding," *Theology* 58, (1955).

An Existentialist Theology: A Comparison of Heidegger and Bultmann. London: SCM Press; New York: Macmillan, 1955. Second Edition, with foreword by Rudolf Bultmann. London: SCM Press; New York: Harper & Row, 1965. Third Edition. London: Penguin Books, 1972.

Helmut Thielicke, "Reflections on Bultmann's Hermeneutic," Translated by John Macquarrie, *The Expository Times* 67 (1956)

"Demonology and the Classic Idea of Atonement," *The Expository Times* 68 (1956).

"A New Kind of Demythologizing?" *Theology* 59 (1956).

"Bultmann's Existential Approach to Theology." *Union Seminary Quarterly Review.* (1957).

"Changing Attitudes to Religion in Contemporary English Philosophy," *The Expository Times,* 68 (1957).

"The Service of Theology," *The Reformed and Presbyterian World* 25 (1958).

"Demythologizing and the Gospel," *The Chaplain* 16 (1959).

"Modern Issues in Biblical Studies: Christian Existentialism," *The Expository Times* 71 (1960).

The Scope of Demythologizing: Bultmann and His Critics. London: SCM Press, New York: Harper & Row, 1960.

"The Natural Theology of Teilhard de Chardin," *The Expository Times* 72 (1961).

"Existentialism and the Christian Vocabulary," *The London Quarterly and Holborn Review* 186 (1961).

History and the Christ of Faith, *The Listener* 67 (1962).

Martin Heidegger, *Being and Time,* Translated by John Macquarrie and Edward Robinson. London: SCM Press; New York: Harper & Row, 1962.

"How is Theology Possible?" *Union Seminary Quarterly Review* 18 (1963).

"Theologians of our Time: Karl Rahner, S. J." *The Expository Times* 74 (1963).

"True Life in Death," *The Journal of Bible and Religion* 21 (1963).

"Beelzebub" and other entries, In *Hastings' Dictionary of the Bible,* 2d ed., ed., F.C. Grant and H.H. Rowley. Edinburgh: T. & T. Clark, 1963.

Twentieth-Century Religious Thought: The Frontiers of Philosophy and Theology, 1900–1960. New York: Harper & Row; and London: SCM Press, 1963. Second Edition, with additional chapter 1960–70. London: SCM Press, 1971. Third Edition with Postscript, 1960–1980. New York: Charles Scribner's Sons, 1981.

Twentieth-Century Religious Thought, Spanish Edition (*El Pensamiento Religioso en el Siglo XX: Las Fronteras de la Filosofia y la Teologia 1900*–1970, translated from the Second English Edition by Juan Estruch. Barcelona: Editorial Merder, 1975.

"Second Thoughts: The Philosophical School of Logical Analysis," *The Expository Times,* 75 (1963).

"Christianity and Other Faiths," *Union Seminary Quarterly Review,* 20 (1964).

"The Problem of Natural Theology," *Pittsburgh Perspective,* 5 (1964).

"Christianity and Other Faiths" [A Rejoinder] *Union Seminary Quarterly Review* 20 (1965).

"Rudolf Bultmann," In *A Handbook of Christian Theologians,* ed. M.E. Marty and D.G. Peerman. Cleveland: World Publishing, 1965.

"A Dilemma in Christology," *The Expository Times* 76 (1965).

"How Can We Think of God?" *Theology Today* 22 (1965).

"Benediction of the Blessed Sacrament," *Ave* 34 (1965).

Studies in Christian Existentialism: Lectures and Essays. Montreal: McGill University Press, 1965. London: SCM Press; Philadelphia: Westminster Press, 1966.

"Philosophy and Theology in Bultmann's Thought," In *The Theology of Rudolf Bultmann,* ed. C.W. Kegley. New York: Harper & Row, 1966.

"God and Secularity," *Holy Cross Magazine* 77 (1966).

"Mother of the Church" [a poem] *Holy Cross Magazine,* 77 (1966).

"The Preexistence of Jesus Christ," *The Expository Times,* 77 (1966).

"The Tri-Unity of God" A reply to P.H. Lehman. *Union Seminary Quarterly Review,* 21 (1966).

Principles of Christian Theology. New York: Charles Scribner's Sons; London: SCM Press, 1966. Second Edition, revised and enlarged. New York: Charles Scribner's Sons; London: SCM Press, 1977.

Principles of Christian Theology, Dutch Edition (*De Beginselen van de christelijke Theologie*). 3 vols. Translated from the First English Edition by Jos Mertens. Roermond: J.J. Romen & Zonen, 1968.

"Some Thoughts on Heresy." *Christianity and Crisis* 26 (1966).

"Heidegger's Earlier and Later Work Compared." *Anglican Theological Review,* 49 (1967).

"Stations of the Cross," *Ave,* 36 (1967).

"Subjectivity and Objectivity in Theology and Worship," *Worship,* 41 (1967).

"Maurice Blondel" and other entries. In *The Encyclopedia of Philosophy.* 8 vols., ed. Paul Edwards. New York: Macmillan and Free Press, 1967.

God-Talk: An Examination of the Language and Logic of Theology. New York: Harper & Row; London: SCM Press, 1967.

God-Talk, Italian Edition (*Ha Senso Parlare di Dio?*) Translated by Giancarlo Rocca. Turin: Borla, 1969.

God-Talk, German Edition (*Gott-Rede: Eine Untersuchung der Sprache und Logik der Theologie*). Translated by Annemarie Pieper, Wurzburg: Echter Verlag, 1974.

God-Talk, Spanish Edition (*God-Talk: el analisis del lenguaje y la logica de la teologia*). Translated by M.B. Garrido. Salamanca: Ediciones Sigueme 1976.

"Faith, Worship, Life." *Holy Cross Magazine* 78 (1967).

"I Recommend You To Read: Some Recent Books on Theology," *The Expository Times* 78 (1967).

Editor and contributor. *Realistic Reflections on Church Union.* Albany: Argus-Greenwood, 1967.

"New Ways in Moral Theology." *The Nashotah Quarterly Review* 7, (1967).

"Divine Omnipotence." *Proceedings of the Seventh Inter-American Congress of Philosophy.* Quebec: Laval University Press, 1967.

"The New Man and the Christian Ethic." *St. Luke's Journal.* 11 (1967).

God and Secularity. Philadelphia: Westminster Press; London: Lutterworth Press, 1967.

God and Secularity. Spanish Edition (*Dios y la Secularidad*). Translated by C.R. Garrido. San Jose: Centro de Publicaciones Cristianas, 1969.

God and Secularity. Japanese Edition (*Kami to konoyo*). Translated by Hiroki Funamoto. Tokyo: Shinkyo Shuppansha Publishing, 1971.

"A Look at the New Theology." Cincinnati: Forward Movement Publications, 1967.

Editor and contributor, *A Dictionary of Christian Ethics.* London: SCM Press; Philadelphia: Westminster Press, 1967.

"Will and Existence." In *The Concept of Willing,* ed. J.N. Lapsley. Nashville: Abingdon Press, 1967.

"Existentialism and Christian Thought." In *Philosophical Resources for Christian Thought,* ed. Perry LeFevre. Nashville: Abingdon Press, 1968.

Editor and contributor. *Contemporary Religious Thinkers: From Idealist Metaphysicians to Existential Theologians.* New York: Harper & Row; London: SCM Press, 1968.

Martin Heidegger. London: Lutterworth Press; Richmond: John Knox Press, 1968.

"The Holy Spirit and the Church," *Holy Cross Magazine* 79 (1968).

"Bultmann's Understanding of God." *The Expository Times* 79 (1968).

"The Doctrine of Creation and Human Responsibility." In *Knowledge and the Future of Man,* ed. W.J. Ong, S.J. New York: Holt, Rinehart & Winston, 1968.

"Karl Barth" and other entries. *A Dictionary of Christian Theology,* ed. Alan Richardson. London: SCM Press, 1969.

"Some Comments on the Trial Liturgy." *American Church Quarterly* 6 (1969).

"Priesthood and the Trial Liturgy." In *Towards a Living Liturgy,* ed. D.L. Garfield. New York: Church of St. Mary the Virgin, 1969.

"What's Next in Theology?" *The Tower,* Union Seminary Alumni Magazine (Spring 1969).

"The Nature of Theological Language." In *Lambeth Essays on Faith*, ed. A.M. Ramsey. London: SPCK, 1969.

"Prayer Is Thinking." *Eucharist*, 8 (1969).

"Schleiermacher Reconsidered." *The Expository Times*, 80 (1969).

"Religious Language and Recent Analytical Philosophy," *Concilium* 6 (1969).

"Secular Ecumenism." *The American Ecclesiastical Review*, 161 (1969).

"Self-Transcending Man." *Commonweal* 91 (1969).

"The Ministry and the Proposed New Anglican-Methodist Ordinal." *The Anglican*, 25 (1969).

"What Still Separates Us from the Catholic Church? An Anglican Reply." *Concilium*, 6 (1970).

Three Issues in Ethics. New York: Harper & Row; London: SCM Press, 1970.

Three Issues in Ethics, Japanese Edition (*Gendai rinri no soten*). Translated by Yasuo Furuya, Tokyo: Jordan Publishing Company, 1973.

"Eschatology and Time." In *The Future of Hope*, ed. Frederick Herzog, New York: Herder & Herder, 1970.

"What is the Gospel?" *The Expository Times* 81 (1970).

"On Gods and Gardeners" In *Perspectives in Education, Religion and the Arts*, ed., H.E. Kiefer and M.K. Munitz. Albany: State University of New York Press, 1970.

"Eucharistic Presence." In *Worship in Spirit and Truth*, ed., D.L. Garfield. New York: Church of St. Mary the Virgin, 1970.

"Word and Idea" *International Journal for the Philosophy of Religion* 1 (1970).

"Is Organic Union Desirable?" *Theology* 73 (1970).

"Theologies of Hope: A Critical Examination" *The Expository Times* 82 (1971).

"A Modern Scottish Theologian: Ian Henderson, 1910–69" *The Expository Times* 82 (1971).

"The Humanity of Christ" *Theology* 74 (1971).

Martin Heidegger, "From the Last Marburg Lecture Course." Translated by John Macquarrie. In *The Future of Our Religious Past: Essays in Honor of Rudolf Bultmann*, ed., James Robinson. London: SCM Press, 1971.

"Martin Heidegger," In *Twelve Makers of Modern Protestant*

Thought, ed. G.L. Hunt. New York: Association Press, 1971.

"Creation and Environment" *The Expository Times* 83 (1971).

"Pluralism in Religion" *Veritas* 3 (1972).

Paths in Spirituality. london: SCM Press; New York: Harper & Row, 1972.

Paths in Spirituality. Japanese Edition (*Reihai to inori no honshitsu*). Translated by Osumi Keizo. Tokyo: Jordan Publishing Company, 1976.

"The Problem of God Today." London: Christian Evidence Society, 1972.

"Anglican-Methodist Dialogue on the Unification of Ministries," *Concilium* 4 (1972).

Existentialism. Philadelphia: Westminster Press; London: Hutchinson, 1972, Second Edition, London and Baltimore: Penguin Books, 1973.

"John McLeod Campbell, 1800–72." *The Expository Times,* 83 (1972).

"Anglicanism and Ecumenism." In *Anglicanism and Principles of Christian Unity,* ed., F.T. Kingston. Windsor, Ontario: Canterbury College, 1972.

"Liberal and Radical Theologies: An Historical Comparison." *The Modern Churchman,* 15 (1972).

"God and the World: Two Realities or One?" *Theology* 75 (1972).

The Faith of the People of God: A Lay Theology. New York: Charles Scribner's Sons; London: SCM Press, 1972.

"The Real God and Real Prayer." In *The British Churches Turn to the Future,* ed. D.L. Edwards. London: SCM Press, 1973.

"What Place Has Individual Conscience in Christianity?" In New Series, Part 1 of *Asking Them Questions,* ed. R.S. Wright. London: Oxford University Press, 1973.

"A Theology of Alienation." In *Alienation: Concept, Term and Meanings,* ed. Frank Johnson. New York: Seminar Press, 1973.

"The Struggle of Conscience for Authentic Selfhood." In *Conscience, Theological and Psychological Perspectives,* ed. C.E. Nelson. New York: Newman Press, 1973.

The Concept of Peace. London: SCM Press; New York: Harper & Row, 1973.

"Women and Ordination: A Mediating View." In *Sexualty, Theology, Priesthood*, ed. H.K. Lutge. San Gabriel, California: Concerned Fellow Episcopalians, 1973.

Mystery and Truth. Milwaukee: Marquette University, 1973.

"Theology." *Encyclopedia Americana*, New York, 1973.

"Kenoticism Reconsidered." *Theology* 77 (1974).

"What Kind of Unity?" *Faith and Unity* 18 (1974).

"Ethical Standards in World Religions: Christianity." *The Expository Times*, 85 (1974).

"Some Reflections on Freedom." *The University Forum*, Charlotte: University of North Carolina, 1974.

"The Hundredth Archbishop of Canterbury." *New Divinity*, 4 (1974).

"Whither Theology?" In *Great Christian Centuries to Come*, ed., C. Martin. London and Oxford: Mowbrays, 1974.

"What a Theologian Expects from the Philosopher." In *The Impact of Belief*, ed. George F. McLean. Lancaster: Concorde Publishing Company, 1974.

"Some Problems of Modern Christology." *The Indian Journal of Theology*, 23 (1974).

"Burns: Poet, Prophet, Philosopher." *The Expository Times*, 86 (1975).

Thinking About God. London: SCM Press; New York: Harper & Row, 1975.

"The Nature of the Marriage Bond." *Theology*, 78 (1975).

Christian Unity and Christian Diversity. London: SCM Press; Philadelphia: Westminster Press, 1975.

"God and the Feminine," *The Way*, Supplement 25 (1975).

"The Uses of Diversity." *The Tablet* (1975).

"The Meeting of Religions in the Modern World: Opportunities and Dangers." *The Journal of Dharma*, 1 (1975).

"The Idea of a Theology of Nature." *Union Seminary Quarterly Review*, 30 (1975).

"The Importance of Belief." *New Fire*, 3 (1975).

"New Thoughts on Benediction." *Ave*, 44 (1975).

"On the Idea of Transcendence." *Encounter and Exchange*, Bulletin 14 (1975).

"The Church and Ministry." *The Expository Times* 87 (1976).

"Priestly Character." In *To Be A Priest*, ed., R.E. Terwilliger and U.T. Holmes. New York: Seabury Press, 1975.

"Authority in Anglicanism." *Agnus Dei*, 2 (1976).

"Recent Thinking on Christian Beliefs: Christology." *The Expository Times* 88 (1976).

"Unity." In *The Upper Room Disciplines, 1977*, ed. Ruth Coffman *et al.*, Nashville: The Upper Room, 1976.

"Rest and Restlessness in Christian Spirituality." In *Spirit and Light*, ed., W.B. Green and Madeleine L'Engle. New York: Seabury Press, 1976.

"Why Believe." *Hullingdon Papers*, 1 (1976).

"A Magnificent Achievement of the Christian Intellect." *Religious Media Today*, 1 (1976).

"Philosophy and Religion in the Nineteenth and Twentieth Centuries: Continuities and Discontinuities." *The Monist*, 60 (1977).

"Christianity Without Incarnation? Some Critical Comments." In *The Truth of God Incarnate*, ed., Michael Green. London: Hodder & Stoughton, 1977.

"Pride in the Church." *Communio*, 4 (1977).

"Death and Eternal Life." *The Expository Times*, 88 (1977).

"The Bishop and Theologians." In *Today's Church and Today's World*, ed., John Howe. London: CIO Publishing, 1977.

The Humility of God: Christian Meditations. London: SCM Press; Philadelphia: Westminister Press, 1978.

The Humility of God. Italian Edition (*L'Umilta de Dio: Meditazione sul mistero della salvezza cristiana*). Translated by Bruno Pistocchi. Milan: Jaca Book, 1979.

"The Significance of Jesus Christ Today." Toronto: Anglican Book Centre, 1978.

"Christian Reflections on Death." *St. Francis Burial Society Quarterly* 2 (1978).

"Faith in Jesus Christ." *Christian World* 1 (1978).

"Religious Experience." *Humanities* 12 (1978).

"The One and the Many: Complementarity of Religions." In *Meeting of Religions*, ed., Thomas Aykara. Bangalore: Dharmaram Publications, 1978.

"The Recognition of Ministries." *Christian World*, 1 (1978).

Christian Hope. London: Mowbray; New York: Seabury Press, 1978.

"The Purposes of Reservation." *The Server*, 11 (1978).

"On the Ordination of Women to the Priesthood." In *Report of the Lambeth Conference, 1978,* ed., Michael Perry. London: CIO Publishing, 1978.

"Immaculate Conception." London: Ecumenical Society of the Blessed Virgin Mary, 1979.

"Existentialism and Theological Method." *Communio,* 6 (1979).

"The Aims of Christianity." *USA Today,* 108 (1979).

"The Humility of God." In *The Myth/Truth of God Incarnate,* ed., D.R. McDonald. Wilton, CT: Morehouse-Barlow, 1979.

"Foundation Documents of the Faith: The Chalcedonian Definition." *The Expository Times,* 91 (1979).

"Commitment and Openness: Christianity's Relation to Other Faiths." *Theology Digest,* 27 (1979).

"Transcendent Belief." In *Science, Faith and Revelation,* ed. R.E. Patterson. Nashville, TN: Broadman Press, 1979.

"Pilgrimage in Theology." *Epworth Review,* 7 (1980).

"Tradition, Truth and Christology." *The Heythrop Journal,* 21 (1980).

"Today's Word for Today; Jurgen Moltmann." *The Expository Times,* 92 (1980).

"God in Experience and Argument." In *Experience, Reason and God,* ed., Eugene T. Long. Washington, D.C." Catholic University of America Press, 1980.

"Religion" and other entries. In *Academic American Encyclopedia.* Princeton, N.J.: Arete Publishing Company, 1980.

"Why Theology?" In *Religious Studies and Public Examinations,* ed., E. Hulmes and B. Watson. Oxford: Farmington Institute, 1980.

"Systematic Theology and Biblical Studies." *Kairos,* no. 2 (1980).

"Truth in Christology." In *God Incarnate: Story and Belief,* ed., A.E. Harvey. London: S.P.C.K., 1981.

"The Concept of a Christ-Event." In *God Incarnate: Story and Belief,* ed. A.E. Harvey. London: S.P.C.K., 1981.

"Glorious Assumption." Walsingham Parish Church, 1981.

"A Generation of Demythologizing." In *Theolinguistics,* ed. J. van Noppen. Brussels: Free University, 1981.

"Existentialist Christology." In *Christological Perspectives,* ed. R.E. Berkey and S.A. Edwards. New York: Pilgrim Press, 1982.

"The End of Empiricism." *Union Seminary Quarterly Review* 37 (1982).

"Being and Giving." In *God: The Contemporary Discussion,* ed., F. Sontag and M.D. Bryant. New York: Rose of Sharon Press, 1982.

"Aspects of the Human Being." *The Virginia Seminary Journal* 34 (1982).

"Structures for Unity." In *Their Lord and Ours,* ed., M. Santer. London: S.P.C.K., 1982.

In Search of Humanity. London: SCM Press, 1982; New York: Crossroads, 1983.

"The Need for a Lay Ministry." *The Times Higher Education Supplement* no. 529 (1982).

"The Future of Anglo-Catholicism." *Church Times* no. 6275 (1983).

"William Temple: Philosopher, Theologian, Churchman." In *The Experiment of Life* ed., F.K. Hare. Toronto: Toronto University Press, 1983.

"God" and other entries. In *Funk & Wagnall's New Encyclopedia.* New York: Funk & Wagnall, 1983.

"Being" and other entries. In *A Dictionary of Christian Spirituality,* ed., Gordon Wakefield. London: SCM Press, 1983.

In Search of Deity. An Essay in Dialectical Theism. The Gifford Lectures delivered at the University of Saint Andrews in session 1983–84. London: SCM Press, 1984.

Index